YOU'RE HIRED!

TOTAL JOB SEARCH 2013

YOU'RE HIRED!

TOTAL JOB SEARCH 2013

JEREMY I'ANSON

You're Hired! Total Job Search 2013

This first edition published in 2012 by Trotman Publishing, an imprint of Crimson Publishing Ltd, Westminster House, Kew Road, Richmond, Surrey TW9 2ND.

© Trotman Publishing 2012

Author: Jeremy I'Anson

British Library Cataloguing in Publication Data
A catalogue record for this book is available from the British Library.

ISBN 978 1 84455 529 1

Typeset by IDSUK (DataConnection) Ltd
Printed and bound in Great Britain by Ashford Colour Press, Gosport, Hants

CONTENTS

ABOUT THE AUTHOR

Jeremy I'Anson is Managing Director of xlSys Consulting, a company focussed on providing career coaching to help individuals, both in and out of work, to maximise their career potential and to plan and prepare for their next career move.

Jeremy spent many years working in senior management roles in the Middle East, latterly as General Manager of a training and development company operated in partnership with BAE Systems and based in Saudi Arabia. On his return to the UK he took up a senior position in Executive Search working with clients in a wide range of business sectors across the EMEA Region. In 2008 Jeremy established his own careers consultancy and has since worked on a one-to-one basis with hundreds of individuals at every level from graduate to CEO who need professional help to find and win their next job.

Jeremy writes regularly on career-related topics and is a regular contributor to national publications including *Computer Weekly* where he also provides careers advice to job seekers.

Jeremy has a Master's Degree in Education from Aston University in birmingham and, in addition to his career coaching, still travels on a regular basis to present management training courses in the Middle East.

Readers can follow Jeremy on Twitter at @totaljobsearch and subscribe to his blog at www.totaljobsearchonline.com where further job search resources and CV templates are available.

Acknowledgements

Thanks to my wife and to my girls for their support and understanding while I worked on *Total Job Search*. Thanks also to everyone at Trotman Publishing for their invaluable advice and support. It takes a team.

INTRODUCTION

Let me tell you a story.

John's an experienced manager with a good degree in economics.
He's a qualified accountant and he's been searching for a new job for
6 months. During that time he's applied for over 50 jobs. He hasn't had a
single interview.

John's a bright guy who has been working continuously since he qualified.
He's hardly ever had to search for work; his previous jobs always came to him
through his network of former colleagues, friends from the golf club and the
occasional headhunter. He's always been in work.

I asked John to send me his CV. It was a bland affair that he had cobbled
together from the job descriptions of each of his jobs over the last 15 years.
A collection of dull facts and figures about the teams he'd led and the policies
and procedures he'd developed. Nowhere in the CV did he refer to the value
that he'd created for his employers, the financial targets he'd achieved or his
expertise in cost reduction and risk management. There was nothing in his CV
that would convince a recruiter or potential employer that he was *the* applicant
to call in for interview.

Even worse, when I looked at the jobs that he'd applied for I knew immediately
that, with a little knowledge and some extra effort, he *could* have been shortlisted
for each of those jobs. He had the skills, experience and qualifications required
but he just hadn't made it clear in his job applications. When I explained why he
hadn't been shortlisted for interviews John realised that finding his next job was
going to be a serious business. He needed to up his game.

John's new full-time job was to find a job. That meant going to the 'office'
every day and spending at least 8 hours researching and preparing his job
applications and customising his CV to ensure that he provided real evidence
of all the skills and experience required by the employer. His new objective
was to be shortlisted for *every* job that he applied for. No more scattergun job
applications with the same old CV.

With the certainty that he was going to be shortlisted for jobs, the question of job interviews arose. The last time John had attended a proper interview was 10 years ago and that was with a client who knew him well. John realised that he'd need to up his game in the interview department as well. Ever heard of competency-based interviews? What about critical incident questions? And what about making a presentation to an interview panel or attending an assessment centre? No, he hadn't heard of those types of interview questions and he hadn't made a formal presentation for years; and he was scared stiff by the thought of attending an assessment centre.

As a professional executive search consultant I speak to people like John almost every day. It's a very typical story for the large number of people searching for jobs, not just in the UK but all over the world.

There are thousands of people looking for work at any one time and yet, judging by the job applications that I receive, only a tiny percentage of those job hunters truly understand the dynamics of a professional job search. People who would have no problem negotiating business deals or managing sales and advertising campaigns for their employers just don't know how to sell themselves.

Now the picture I've painted may not fit your circumstances exactly but I'm guessing that you've picked up this book because you are searching for a job and you'd like some advice and support to ensure that you get offered that job as quickly and as painlessly as possible.

Regardless of your personal situation or your professional level, the business of finding the right job in the current recruitment market is going to be a challenging and sometimes frustrating experience. But, despite the gloomy economic outlook, there *are* jobs available. There are roles in almost every job category advertised in the newspapers each week. On a single internet site in the UK there are currently over 350,000 vacancies. And yet many very well qualified and experienced people are still struggling to find a new job.

Why is that?

It's simply because employers and recruiters are inundated with CVs, with many advertised vacancies receiving a hundred or more applications. Rather surprisingly many of those applications are of very poor quality. Employers and recruiters frequently comment that even senior-level applications are rejected out of hand because of poorly written CVs and application forms that contain typos, spelling mistakes or bad grammar. In a recent survey, conducted by Robert Half International, 84% of executives said that it takes just one or two typos in a CV to 'remove a candidate from consideration for a position'. Furthermore, many candidates fail to read the job advertisement thoroughly and either do not have the required skills or experience or have not provided proper evidence of their skills or experience that would encourage an employer or recruiter to shortlist them or invite them to interview.

Those recruiters are the individuals who can make or break your job application. That survey highlights just how important it is to have a well written and compelling CV. If your CV looks unprofessional and careless then recruiters or employers will almost certainly conclude that that attitude will also be reflected in your work.

Employers often comment that many of the candidates who *were* invited to a job interview were quickly rejected because they had not undertaken even basic preparation. Complaints from employers include:

- candidates arrive late for the interview
- candidates report to the wrong address
- candidates are inappropriately dressed
- candidates cannot answer even basic questions about the employer's organisation
- candidates cannot provide evidence of their experience for the job
- candidates do not demonstrate commitment to the job
- candidates do not listen to or do not fully answer questions.

All of the above should send a clear message to job hunters. The process of applying for a new job and attending interviews in the current job market is going to be difficult and needs to be treated with the same energy and professionalism that anyone would apply to their actual job. The fact that this is often *not* the case should encourage the readers of this book! The clear implication is that while there is undoubtedly tough competition for jobs, many job hunters fail to put in the time and effort required to properly control the quality of their applications and continue to submit CVs that are either full of errors or do not provide sufficient evidence to support their application. Furthermore, many shortlisted candidates do not prepare for job interviews and then fail to provide satisfactory answers to interview questions.

The purpose of this book is to provide you with an insider's guide to job search that will enable you to write a CV that is properly targeted for each and every job that you apply for. What's more, this book will provide you with a wide range of easily learned techniques that will ensure that you can confidently answer even the toughest interview questions. Along the way you'll learn how to network, how to find unadvertised jobs and how to use the internet and social media to give added impetus to your job search and put you ahead of the competition.

The format of the book follows the actual steps of a typical job search, starting with planning your job search campaign and the production of supporting collateral (your CVs and covering letters) and concluding with powerful techniques that will ensure that you perform at your very best at different types of job interviews, presentations and assessments.

The book also provides advice and guidance on a wide range of related topics including:

- using the right keywords in your CV
- structuring your career achievements
- making outstanding job applications
- dealing with recruitment consultants and headhunters
- developing your two-minute elevator pitch
- answering the toughest interview questions
- dealing with assessment centres.

This book is different from many of the current crop of CV and interview books. It is not a list of old recruiters' anecdotes, bland CV templates or stock interview responses. Instead I provide workable models, tools and techniques that you can use immediately to plan your job search, create a powerful CV, write great covering letters, use social media (such as LinkedIn, Facebook and Twitter) to build your network, and effectively pitch your skills to your contacts. I'll also show you how to prepare for your interviews. How to predict what interview questions you are going to be asked. How to find out what the employer is *really* looking for. I'll also show you how to impress the interviewers with the quality of your own questions.

You can pick any chapter as a stand-alone guide depending on your personal circumstances. If you've got an interview coming up then go straight to Chapter 6 on interview preparation. If you are getting no response to your job applications then you almost certainly need to look at the chapters on creating a CV and making job applications.

This book is intended for *anyone* looking for a job. The examples used throughout the book refer to a range of different roles in different job categories and at different levels of experience. The advice given can apply to job hunters at any stage in their careers. So whether you are a school leaver, recent graduate, intern, middle manager or CEO, you will find advice here that is relevant to *your* job search.

Remember that 90% of the candidates applying for *your* job will not have had access to the insider's tips and techniques provided in this book. Simply follow the advice provided in each chapter to ensure that you give yourself a head start, stand out from the crowd and ultimately get the job that you really want.

1 PLANNING YOUR JOB SEARCH

Many people faced with the task of searching for a new job tend to jump straight in and send off their CV and make as many job applications as they can. In this chapter I'll suggest that before embarking on your job search and starting to make any actual job applications you should step back and carefully plan your job search strategy. Of course you need to think about the kinds of jobs you will apply for, but you also need to put in place a few simple strategies that will enable you to conduct your job search efficiently and effectively.

This chapter will help you:

■ manage yourself to ensure that you are focusing on the right job search activities

■ measure your progress against some specific and timed job search goals

■ set up and equip your home office

- decide which jobs you will apply for

- use any spare time to upgrade your qualifications and training

- decide *how* you will go about finding your next job.

Getting started

Before embarking on your job search you should consider *how* you are going to manage and plan your search. Of course there will be the practical side to the search. You will need a good CV (or résumé), a selection of jobs to consider and an excellent covering letter. In addition, you will need to prepare carefully for interviews. All of these topics will be dealt with in detail in later chapters of this book, along with all the other stages of your job search.

The first key step is to get a good positive attitude. You need to be determined to succeed. You have a unique set of skills, experiences and achievements that will be of real value to your next employer. Some people become disheartened when they have been made redundant (or laid off) or when they have applied for many jobs without success. By following the steps detailed in this book you will set out on the right path, and your CV and job applications will be a great deal better than those of the vast majority of the people applying for jobs. You *will* be successful and you *will* find the job that you really want!

TOTAL JOB SEARCH TIP

Get yourself in a positive frame of mind!

Managing yourself

As you will be managing your search as a professional job search campaign, the most important factor in that campaign will be managing yourself. It's important that you develop the habit of 'going to work' each day. Assuming that you are not actually working, then being 'job search campaign manager' is your new full-time job.

As with any job, you will need to plan your week and keep a well structured 'to do' list of daily activities. If you have access to applications such as

Microsoft Office and Outlook then you will be able to create a task list in the calendar – and, of course, place reminders for calls and meetings. Use a spreadsheet application (such as Microsoft Excel) to record all your job applications, telephone conversations and interviews. All of this activity takes a lot of discipline, and for someone who is not used to working at home it is easy to become distracted. How nice it would be to take the dog for a walk, stroll to the shops or watch some daytime television! The best way to counter the temptation to lose concentration is to set yourself some clear daily targets and deadlines.

Some people find it helpful to divide the day up into one-hour sessions. You can dedicate a set period of time each day for research, searching for jobs on the internet, making actual job applications and so on. In addition to this you will be making phone calls to people who may be able to help you to find your next job. These people could be members of your family, friends, neighbours and colleagues, all of whom may potentially become part of your network of contacts who may be able to help you directly or indirectly to find a job. Additionally you will need to put aside some time to follow up on any introductions or referrals that you receive from these contacts. The process of networking will be covered in detail in Chapter 4.

Then you will need to factor in time for face-to-face meetings or interviews with recruiters, network contacts and, of course, potential employers. Try to make the best use of your time when arranging to meet recruiters and contacts. It makes sense to schedule a number of meetings on a single day so that you save valuable time and money on the cost of travel.

If you are still working, then finding the time to search for a new job will be that much more difficult. If you have been made redundant and you are working out your notice then your employer should allow you some time off to attend interviews but you may still need to spend additional time to ensure a successful job search. Can you access the internet during your commute to work? Could you agree with your family to spend at least two evenings a week at home on job search activities? Can you spend Saturday and Sunday mornings reading the appointments sections of the newspapers and applying for jobs?

Set your job search goals

Any well run campaign should have some clear goals established at the outset. At the risk of bringing up distant memories of dull management training courses, those goals should be **SMART**.

- **S**pecific
- **M**easurable
- **A**chievable
- **R**ealistic
- **T**ime limited

It makes sense to be quite specific about your ultimate goal, and it's always worth writing it down.

Here's a **specific** goal as it relates to your job search:

'I intend to find a new job as an IT manager.'

If you are currently an experienced IT manager then that objective would seem to be specific, measurable, achievable and realistic.

However, that goal lacks one key element – it needs to be time limited.

Any project manager will tell you that planning a project without a clear end date is a recipe for disaster. The project will not be completed satisfactorily.

So let's add that timescale to the job search goal.

'I intend to find a new job as an IT manager within 12 weeks.'

That's a lot better.

TOTAL JOB SEARCH TIP

Use SMART goals in your job search.

But don't set unrealistic objectives!

A number of job hunters, unfortunately, do not have realistic objectives – that is one of the key reasons why their job search campaigns fail. Current statistics indicate that job hunters typically take from 3 to 6 months to find a new job, so being realistic about timescales is important. Another key factor is the type of job, that you are applying for. When there are a significant number of applications for a particular job, employers will be able to be very selective when making their shortlist.

Only apply for jobs where you have most or preferably all of the skills required. That's realistic.

Set short-term goals

In order to achieve your ultimate goal of finding a new job within a set timeframe you will need to establish short-term goals along the way.

Set yourself some job search milestones, for example:

- get your new CV completed at the end of week one of your job search campaign
- call at least five of your contacts in week one
- respond to at least five job advertisements by the end of week two
- attend at least three interviews by the end of week four.

An essential element of the SMART objective model is that your progress towards your goal should be measurable. In the course of your job search campaign there will be many activities that you can measure. These activities could include:

- the number of job applications you intend to make every day or every week
- the number of phone calls you plan to make to recruiters and potential employers
- the number of responses you receive from your applications
- the number of meetings with recruiters
- the number of networking events that you attend
- the number of first interviews that you attend
- the number of second or final interviews that you attend.

TOTAL JOB SEARCH TIP

Use a spreadsheet to keep track of your activities.

Establish your home office

If you have the space, set up a home office with everything that you need to conduct a professional job search. Even if this is the kitchen table you need to 'go to the office' every day.

Your home office should include the following equipment.

A computer connected to the internet

This is going to be essential for your job search. You need to be able to search for jobs on the internet and of course send out emailed or online job applications. Even if you don't have access to the internet or a computer at home, you should be able to use the facilities in your local library or at a local job centre or internet café.

A word processing application

You will also need a good word processing application. Microsoft Word is the most commonly used package; beware of other packages that create files that recruiters may not be able to view or where the formatting might be affected. The best way to guarantee that your CV and application letter look as you intend is to send the file in a **PDF format**. This will guarantee the correct appearance of your CV and ensure that it is not changed in any way. If you are not sure how to do this you can find plenty of free downloads on the internet that will convert documents to the PDF format. You can find further details in Chapter 10.

A good-quality printer

Although you will be making most of your job applications either by email or online, you may still need to send the occasional hard-copy application. Printers are relatively cheap these days so make sure the quality of your printed job applications is outstanding. You may also want to print out job specifications and directions for job interviews. If you are using a public computer in an internet café or library it is usually possible to print documents for a small charge.

A job search email address

It's easy to set up a new email address – even if you already have one you should consider setting up a dedicated address for your job search. This way you know that every email coming in to that address is related to your job search and there will be no chance of mixing up personal and business emails. Don't use silly email addresses (i.e. fluffy.bunny@email.com); keep it straight and professional. You can set up a free email address using providers such as Hotmail and Gmail.

A job search telephone

Have you considered getting a dedicated phone and phone number for your job search? A cheap mobile and a pay-as-you-go (prepaid) SIM card is all you need. Now you will know that any calls coming through on that phone will be related to your job search. Recruiters often call for an impromptu interview and you don't want to be caught in the supermarket queue when they call. Have a polite, professional voicemail message (not the jokey one on your personal phone) and have the certainty that when you answer your job search phone it's going to be an important call and needs to be answered professionally.

Business cards

Since you are going to be networking and meeting people in the course of your job search it's a good idea to get some business cards printed. These can be simple cards that provide just your contact details. This is going to be so much more professional than having to constantly write down your contact details on scraps of paper.

Which jobs should I apply for?

At the outset start thinking about the kinds of jobs that you intend to apply for. If you are just starting out in your career or still studying, consider talking to a careers adviser about the careers you are interested in and the options open to you. If you are already working then are you looking for a very similar job to the one you already have? Are you looking for a more senior role with greater responsibility? Are you thinking of applying for a different kind of job, perhaps in a completely different sector? Remember that in this very competitive job market, making a complete career change will be very tough. More often than not employers will favour candidates who have previous experience in their field. Nevertheless, if you are truly determined then it is certainly possible to change direction at any point in your career.

What kind of company or organisation?

Are you looking to work for a large or small company? If you have been working in the public sector and are now finding that there are limited opportunities, have you got transferable skills that would enable you to find work in the private sector? What are those transferable skills?

What location?

Are you willing to relocate or perhaps consider a longer commute? If you have been lucky enough to have been working close to home, don't assume that you will be able to find a similar job near your home now. The more flexible you can be on the job location, the greater the number of opportunities that will be open to you.

Working overseas

When markets are tough in the UK, many companies consider exporting their products to more receptive markets overseas. In the same way, if you can't find a ready market for your skills in the UK, have you considered working overseas? The job market may be tough in your own country but there may still be plenty of opportunities in other countries. A period spent working overseas can often be a plus factor when you return home. Some of the benefits might include a better salary (tax-free in some countries) and very often the opportunity to take on greater responsibilities. If *exporting* your skills is an option, then consider looking at the international sections of some of the internet job sites and don't confine your job search to your own country. You can search for jobs in specific countries by visiting the world's largest internet job site at www.monster.com or by using a search engine such as Google to find job sites in the countries you are interested in. Remember that if you are a citizen of the European Union then you are free to work in any of the 27 EU countries. However, before investing time in an overseas job search, do check the procedures for obtaining a work permit and make sure that you are potentially eligible to work in the country (or countries) that you select.

What salary/package?

Will you be looking for a similar salary package to the one you have currently? For the right position would you consider a slightly lower package initially? If you are looking for your first permanent role, think about what sort of salary you need and then do some research to ensure your expectations are realistic. Don't undersell yourself and remember to take into account the cost of your commute if the job on offer is further from home than your current role. Be realistic and establish your market value by viewing roles advertised in the press and on internet job sites. Setting salary expectations too high can be one reason why job hunters sometimes struggle to find a new job.

Once you have decided on your salary and benefits package, do make sure that you state this very clearly when you are applying for jobs either directly with an employer or through a recruitment agency. Sometimes the salary package will be stated in the job advertisement, but if it's not then be very clear about your requirements early in your contacts with a potential employer or recruitment agency. You don't want to waste valuable time applying for a job only to find that the package on offer is much lower than you had expected.

Planning your job search campaign

So you have your home office, you have business cards, a job search phone and a job search email address. You are now ready to actually plan your job search. If you think in terms of a marketing campaign and the launch of a new product (that's you!) then there are some key marketing activities that you will need to undertake at this stage.

The market

In the world of sales and marketing, companies do not launch a new product without first undertaking some market research. In the context of a job search you need to research the potential market for jobs that will be available to you. We have already established that the current job market is very tough but that there are in fact jobs available. The evidence for this is the

number of jobs that are advertised, not to mention the thousands of jobs that are available but are not advertised. Your research at this stage should be to identify if jobs are actually available in your field. Start to look in the press and online and search for jobs that might be suitable for you and which match your skills and experience. Pay particular attention to the section of the advertisement which specifies the 'essential skills and experience' for the job. Do you have the skills and experience required?
Do you have the qualifications required?

Addressing market needs

It is sometimes the case that if you have been working for a particular employer for a period of time, the market will have moved on and there are jobs where a particular qualification (or training) was not a requirement previously but now seems to be essential. There are many examples of this:

- teachers
- IT professionals
- business development specialists
- property managers
- financial advisers/bankers
- HR professionals.

People may have been able to undertake these sorts of jobs without any formal qualifications previously but now many of these jobs *do* require some sort of professional qualification. In fact, recruiters will almost certainly favour job applicants who are formally qualified over unqualified applicants. Furthermore, when there are large numbers of candidates available for jobs then employers can also be more demanding and have the option to employ only well qualified staff.

So now is a very good time to review your own qualifications and training and evaluate these against the current requirements specified in job advertisements for roles that you plan to apply for. If you have some free time then you could undertake some further training. Very often the simple fact that you have enrolled on a training course at your own expense will impress an employer. If you have excellent practical experience in your field but lack a particular qualification then the fact that you have taken steps to rectify that shortfall will always count in your favour.

TOTAL JOB SEARCH TIP

Bring your training and qualifications up to date.

Take a look at two examples of job hunters who made the decision to undertake further training to improve their chances of finding new jobs.

CASE STUDY: IT PROJECT MANAGER

Richard is an experienced IT project manager. He has been successfully managing large and complex IT projects within the retail banking sector for nearly 10 years. He is currently looking for work. Richard reviewed the computer press and the internet job sites and noticed that many of the job advertisements indicated a requirement for 'professionally qualified' project managers. Richard called several of the recruitment agencies who were advertising the jobs. They confirmed that their clients generally required project managers to have either the **PRINCE2** qualification (in the UK) or the **PMP** (project management professional) qualification. They also confirmed that, in the current job market, without one of these qualifications Richard would be unlikely to be considered for a job. Richard found a course for the PMP qualification and immediately signed up for an internet-based part-time course. He added the words 'Currently studying for the PMP qualification' to his CV. This ensured that his CV would be found by recruiters searching databases and using the keyword '**PMP**'. For some recruiters and employers the fact that Richard has good practical experience of project management and is now undertaking the required professional training will ensure that he is shortlisted for jobs.

CASE STUDY: HR MANAGER

Amanda worked as an unqualified HR manager for 10 years. She is an experienced HR professional and, after taking some time out to raise two young children, she is now ready to return to work. Having reviewed recent job advertisements she has noticed that many employers now require a professional HR qualification. She called the HR departments of a number of employers who identified the **CIPD Certificate in HR Practice (CHRP)** as the most suitable qualification in HR management. This qualification has been designed for people with previous experience in HR and was available as a fast-track course. The fact that Amanda has taken the trouble to study for the required qualification will make her a more attractive candidate for many employers. The fact that she is willing to self-fund the training is a very good indication of her level of motivation and commitment to a career in HR. Furthermore, Amanda can add 'Currently studying for the CIPD Certificate in HR Practice (CHRP)' to her CV, which will ensure that recruiters will find her details in a keyword search which includes the terms '**CIPD**' or '**CHRP**'.

Both these case studies are good examples of people demonstrating their determination to get back into work and taking realistic steps to ensure that their skills, training and qualifications are up to date and will match the current requirements of employers in their fields. Before you invest in a training course, check job advertisements and confirm with recruitment agencies and potential employers to make absolutely sure that the qualification or training *will* improve your chances of finding a job. It's often the case that employers will choose a candidate with a qualification over an unqualified alternative candidate but do make sure that you select the right qualification(s) for your target job.

The channels to market

In an effective marketing campaign you need to look at the available channels to market. In other words, the channels that you are going to follow in order to find jobs.

There are six potential job search channels that you can follow:

- jobs advertised in the press
- jobs advertised on the internet
- jobs found through recruitment agencies
- jobs found via your networking activities
- jobs found via social media
- jobs found at recruitment events or career fairs.

Jobs advertised in the press

It's easy to find jobs advertised in the press. All of the daily papers and the weekend papers (e.g. *The Sunday Times* Appointments section in the UK) have vacancies advertised. Don't forget also to check magazines, particularly trade magazines – they not only advertise vacancies but also may provide information about companies that are likely to be expanding and may therefore have job vacancies in the future.

The downside of applying for jobs in the press is that so many other people also find it easy to apply for these jobs. A front-page advertisement in a national newspaper appointments section might easily attract 500 applicants or more. That's a lot of competition.

Jobs advertised on the internet

Again, it's easy to find jobs advertised here. There are hundreds of internet job sites and you can search for jobs using a number of different criteria including job title, job location, salary, job category, sector and so on. Don't forget that many recruitment agencies and executive search consultancies also advertise jobs on their own websites. Additionally, many companies have 'Careers' tabs on their websites so that you can look directly for jobs on the employer's website.

The internet is a great source of jobs at every level. Don't assume that jobs advertised on the internet are only for lower-level roles. That's not the case; there are plenty of very senior executive-level roles advertised on the internet and a number of sites that focus specifically on 'executive' vacancies. The executive search consultancies (e.g. www.odgersberndtson.co.uk) often have vacancies advertised on their websites with salaries in excess of £150,000 per annum. A list of internet job sites can be found in Chapter 10.

The downside of applying for jobs advertised on the internet is the possibility that the job doesn't actually exist! While it is unlikely that an employer would spend thousands of pounds on an expensive newspaper advertisement for a non-existent job, it's very easy for a recruitment agency to place a 'catch-all' cheap advertisement on an internet job site for 'project managers' just to build up their candidate database. Before wasting your time responding to internet advertisements (especially those with rather vague requirements) it's always worth calling up and checking on the role. Equally, be aware that several different recruitment agencies may be advertising the same job for a single client. Don't make the mistake of applying for the same job several times and risk having your CV forwarded to the same client by several different agencies. Look out for job advertisements with very similar wording and always check with the agency to establish the name of the employer before agreeing to have your CV submitted. If the agency won't identify the client then don't let them submit your CV. Of course, make sure you keep a record in your job search spreadsheet of when and where your CV has been submitted.

TOTAL JOB SEARCH TIP

Don't send out duplicate job applications!

Jobs found through recruitment agencies

Because there are so many candidates available, many agencies no longer advertise their clients' jobs. Previously, advertising would have been a major budget item, but now recruitment agencies can count on many candidates registering directly with them. When a client has a new job they can simply search their own internal database for suitable candidates, and email selected vacancies to candidates who are registered with them, so it is certainly worth registering with some of the recruitment agencies. (For a list of recruitment agencies see Chapter 10.)

Look at the press and internet job sites and you will start to build up a picture of which agencies are advertising the jobs that you would like to apply for. It will quickly become apparent that there are agencies that specialise in particular types of jobs. Agencies may specialise in IT, HR, finance, sales and marketing and so on. Call these agencies first and offer to send them your CV and, if possible, make appointments to meet them. Try to identify reliable, individual consultants and stay in touch with them. They will have insider knowledge of the job market and the best consultants will genuinely want to help you find a job (and earn themselves a commission in the process!).

Jobs found via your networking activities and via social media

We'll cover this activity in a lot more detail in Chapter 4. Using your network can be one of the most effective ways of finding a job. The advantage of this channel will be the lack of competition. Through your network you may find new jobs that have not even been advertised. Networking is going to form a very important part of your job search campaign. The various social media platforms, including Twitter, Facebook and LinkedIn, are all tools that you can use to assist your job search. If you have a Twitter account then now would be a good time to Tweet your availability for work to your followers. The same applies to your Facebook friends.

Jobs found at recruitment events or career fairs

There are many different events that you can attend (often for free) where there may be opportunities for you to find your next job. Apart from career fairs (which may be organised by universities) there are also company open days when anyone can turn up and meet recruiters. But you can also attend conferences, seminars and workshops which are run regularly by local chambers of commerce and organisations such as Business Link (www. businesslink.gov.uk). You should also check your local paper plus any relevant trade journals (for your profession); these will also carry announcements about events. Remember to take your business cards and several copies of your CV along to any events.

Your marketing materials

Perhaps the most important element of your job search campaign will be the marketing collateral that you use to sell yourself to the market. In the context of a job search that collateral will include a powerful CV, your application letters, application forms, emails and any other material that you might need to send out to recruiters to secure job interviews. The most important item is your CV, which is the subject of the next chapter.

IN A NUTSHELL

- Maintain a positive attitude towards your job search – you *will* succeed.
- Set **SMART** goals that are specific, measurable, achievable, realistic and time limited.
- Set realistic milestones.
- Track and measure all of your activities on a regular basis.
- Set up a home office and 'go to work' every day.
- Plan your daily and weekly activities.
- Plan which jobs you are going to apply for.
- Use all the six channels to market in your job search.
- Use your free time to undergo further training or obtain further qualifications if necessary.
- Keep track of your job applications to measure your progress and to avoid duplicate CV submissions.

---

2 CREATING A POWERFUL CV

You need a CV to apply for most jobs and yet in my experience many job hunters don't recognise the importance of having a CV that closely matches the specific requirements of the jobs they are applying for. They use the same old CV for every job application. Sending off dozens of job applications and getting no response is a clear indication that your CV is not doing its job. Having a really good, targeted CV will ensure that you *do* get shortlisted and invited to job interviews.

This chapter will help you:

■ understand the purpose of the CV

■ write a clear profile at the beginning of your CV that is properly targeted at the job you are applying for

■ identify the key skills and experience that are essential requirements for the job

- write about your achievements using a structured and easy-to-use model

- use powerful 'action' words to add impact to your CV

- use job advertisements to find the right keywords and phrases that will ensure that your CV is found by recruiters searching for candidates on the internet or on their agency database.

What is the purpose of a CV?

- It attracts the attention of recruiters/employers.
- If well written, it stands out from other CVs.
- It presents your skills and experience clearly and concisely.
- It provides details of your education and qualifications.
- It demonstrates to the employer that you have the necessary experience to do the job.
- It provides evidence of your suitability for the job.
- It provides examples of your professional achievements that are relevant to the employer.
- A properly targeted (and well written) CV will get you interviews.

The last point is the most important.

TOTAL JOB SEARCH TIP

Targeted CVs get you shortlisted for interviews.

Your CV must demonstrate that you have the specific skills, experience and qualifications requested in the job advertisement or job specification. If the job advertisement states 'university degree essential' then, in this tough recruitment market, recruiters will reject all applicants who do not have a university degree. If the essential requirement is for 'previous experience in the investment banking sector' then recruiters will reject all applicants without that experience. You *must* read the job advertisement or job specification carefully and ensure that the experience and qualifications required are clearly shown in your CV. If you are not sure if your experience is relevant then call the recruiter and check.

As a recruiter faced with the task of shortlisting between three and four candidates from a pool of 100 applicants, the best and fairest option is to shortlist only those candidates who can match every part of the job requirement. Very often I hear of people who have sent off dozens of job applications without success. Invariably the reason is that they do not have the skills, experience or qualifications specified in the job advertisement or in the (usually more detailed) job specification.

If a job looks like it is a good fit but the advertisement is short on detail, it is always worth calling the employer or recruiter to double-check for further details of the job specification.

General guidelines for a good CV

Keep it short and clear

The CV should be easy to read and well laid out with clear section headings and with the information presented in a logical and easy-to-follow format.

Keep it relevant

Don't spend a page describing your successful millennium project; it has no relevance for employers today! It's also better not to fill the front page of your CV with details of your school examination results and grades if you have been in employment for some time already. The exception to this rule would be recent graduates; we will look at the layout and content of graduate CVs in more detail later in this chapter (see page 62).

Use a clear and easy-to-read typeface

Remember that many CVs are read on a computer screen these days. What looks good on paper may not be so clear on screen. Arial, Calibri, Garamond, Tahoma, Times Roman and Verdana are all good, clear typefaces suitable for CVs.

Proofread the CV

The biggest cause of rejection of CVs is poor spelling and grammar mistakes. Don't let yourself down by having careless mistakes in your CV. Check carefully yourself, use a spell checker, and then get a friend or colleague to proofread the CV for you.

Be prepared to modify and update your CV

So many people write their CV and then send the same version out with every job application. You should keep modifying and updating your CV. Listen to comments and advice from recruiters and be prepared to make changes. Consider having several different versions of your CV, for example a CV that emphasises your strategic management skills, and another that highlights your operational/practical experience if these are the skills that are being specifically asked for.

How do recruiters review your CV?

Put yourself in the place of a busy recruiter faced with an inbox of a hundred or more job applications and CVs.

It's 8.30a.m. and the client has already been on the phone requesting the 'three best CVs by lunchtime'. That recruiter is under a great deal of pressure to work fast.

Anecdotal evidence suggests that a typical recruiter will take less than 30 seconds to make a decision on whether or not you are a suitable candidate for a job. That initial decision will almost certainly be based, at least in part, on the contents of your **profile** or the **executive summary** at the top of the first page of your CV. The recruiter will most likely be reading your CV on a computer screen, so think in terms of 'screens of information' rather than pages. In practice, when recruiters open your CV document they will probably see only the top half of page one of your CV.

If you fill this space with the words **CURRICULUM VITAE** (in large capital letters) followed by your name and address spread over five or six lines, followed by the names of all your schools and the subjects and grades of all your exam subjects, you will probably have used up all of that valuable space without providing any information that would enable the recruiter to make a decision on whether or not to shortlist you for a job. The recruiter will probably just move on to the next candidate.

Your contact details

It is much better to start your CV with just four lines containing your name, address and contact details.

So the top of your CV should look like this.

Richard Green
128 Reading Lane, Reading, Berkshire RG90 4XX
Telephone: 01234 567891
Email: richard.green@email.com

Building a profile. Who are you? What do you do?

Directly under your contact details you should include your profile. A profile is a short statement that gives a brief summary of who you are and what you do. It should be succinct and easy to read but nevertheless it needs to make a strong impact. If it doesn't then the recruiter will probably not read the rest of your CV! Over the following pages we'll look at profiles for various types of jobs and for candidates at different stages in their careers.

Here are the key components of a good profile.

Who are you?
Your job title, professional status or background.

What do you do?
The unique combination of skills, qualifications and experience that make you right for this particular job.

What are your career objectives?
Here you can state what you are looking for and what you would like to do in the future.

You can start your profile with a phrase like the following, adapting this sentence to suit your own background:

A versatile IT manager with 5 years' experience in the development and delivery of database systems.

Next, pinpoint some key skills and experience. This will focus the recruiter's attention on some of the reasons why you could be right for the job. To return to our example, you could highlight some of your skills, qualifications and experience:

A qualified project manager with excellent experience of Oracle including the Oracle E-Business Suite and with a proven ability to deliver projects on schedule and within budget.

With your background established, you can now state what kind of job you are looking for and where you'd like to take your career in the future:

Seeking a challenging new role working in a fast-moving international environment.

So now your profile might look like this:

A versatile IT manager with 5 years' experience in the development and delivery of database systems. A qualified project manager with excellent experience of Oracle including the Oracle E-Business Suite and with a proven ability to deliver projects on schedule and within budget. Seeking a challenging new role working in a fast-moving international environment.

Your profile should be easy to read and should contain sufficient information for a recruiter to match your skills to a specific job. Be flexible and be prepared to adapt your profile to match the job you are applying for. For example, if the job advertisement stated the job title as 'assistant accountant' and you are an 'accounting technician' but with the same or very similar responsibilities, then consider editing your profile to reflect that title.

TOTAL JOB SEARCH TIP

Use the job title that recruiters will be looking for.

This kind of profile is a good, straightforward model for the first paragraph of a CV targeted at a particular role. It's very important to understand that you cannot send out the same CV for every job application. Customise the profile to ensure that the recruiter sees the skills and experience that they are looking for. Of course you cannot invent skills and experience that you don't have, but most people have a range of experience in different areas. It would be impossible to condense all of that experience into a single paragraph. The key is to select the experience that will be appropriate for the particular job application.

TOTAL JOB SEARCH TIP

Don't send out the same CV for every job!

This advice is fundamental to the model described in this book: if you accept this advice you will be doing something that 90% of job applicants just don't do. No wonder they don't get shortlisted!

Take the time to analyse carefully the job advertisement or job specification, and, if necessary, check the details with the recruiter so that you fully understand what the employer is looking for. That is why you should *not* be sending off dozens of job applications every week. I would recommend spending a significant amount of time customising your CV for just one or two jobs that you *know* you can do and where you have *all* the skills, experience and qualifications required.

You can use the profile template suggested above to develop a strong profile for any job, no matter what your professional background. Try writing out a profile yourself.

WRITE YOUR OWN PROFILE

Who are you?

_____

_____

_____

What do you do?

_____

_____

_____

What are your career objectives?

_____

_____

Now write your full profile here.

_____

_____

_____

_____

_____

_____

_____

_____

_____

_____

Use job advertisements

You can use job advertisements to help you find the right words and phrases to use in your profile. This technique is very powerful and will enable you to easily customise your profile for different jobs. Start by picking several different advertisements from the press or from the internet that are advertising the type of jobs that you would like to apply for. Note down the most important requirements, keywords and phrases. Imagine that you are the recruiter screening CVs for that job. What would you be looking for? Take a look at some of these recent job advertisements for different categories of jobs and the accompanying profiles.

Marketing manager

- Graduate education or equivalent and an established successful marketing professional with 2–3 years' marketing experience, possibly CIM-qualified, personally credible and comfortable managing multiple stakeholders.

- Broad-based experience, in particular of digital marketing, including the development and execution of digital strategy and online CRM in a multiple-channel customer-facing business.

- A background gained in a fast-paced, commercially demanding environment, with a culture of innovation and in which the advanced use of technology to drive customer service and productivity is essential.

- Experience in an organisation where the need for high-integrity customer interaction is critical, as is the ability to react to rapidly changing market conditions.

Your profile could be as follows.

A degree-qualified marketing professional with 3 years' broad experience in multi-channel customer-focused roles. A member of the Chartered Institute of Marketing (MCIM) with an outstanding track record of success working in an innovative and fast-paced commercial environment using online CRM technology. Now seeking a challenging new role in the field of digital marketing.

This profile is built around the same **Who are you?/What do you do?** model that we used previously. There is of course an assumption that this candidate actually does have the skills and experience specified in the advertisement. Remember that if you don't have the skills specified then in today's tough recruitment market you will not get shortlisted.

In this instance, if you are a senior marketing professional with a degree and a qualification from the Chartered Institute of Marketing but you do not have experience in the 'use of technology to drive customer service and productivity', then you should not be applying for this role. That is an essential requirement of the job as spelled out very clearly in the advertisement.

TOTAL JOB SEARCH TIP

Use job advertisements to customise your profile.

Let's look at another example.

Organisational development analyst

This is a newly created HR role that will focus on organisational structure and change management within a fast-paced advertising business.

Key responsibilities
- Working with the organisational development manager to develop new systems and processes to ensure that the business generates best value for money.
- Responsible for optimising organisational structures and systems to improve service and cut costs.

Essential requirements
- Bachelor's degree
- CIPD qualified (preferred)
- Minimum 2 years' experience in organisational development
- Proven ability to work as part of a team

In this advertisement we can see immediately the essential requirements for the job. Any recruiter will start their search by eliminating all candidates who do not have those qualifications and skills. Because of time pressures the recruiter will prefer to see those skills and qualifications immediately at the beginning of the CV. Here's the suggested profile.

A degree-qualified HR professional with 2 years' experience of developing organisational structures and systems. A member of the Chartered Institute of Personnel and Development (MCIPD) with a proven ability to work effectively in a team environment. Now seeking a challenging new role focused on service improvement and value for money.

Again, this profile covers most of the key requirements outlined in the job advertisement and would certainly encourage the recruiter to keep reading the CV.

How good is the profile? Well, it needs to be good enough to encourage the recruiter to read on. If it passes that first very quick check to see if the candidate has at least the basic requirements for the job then it is a good profile. The only purpose of the profile is to persuade the recruiter to continue reading your CV. Now we need to provide a little more detail about your skills and experience to further increase your chances of being shortlisted for the job.

PROFILE CHECKLIST

- Use the Who are you?/What do you do? model.
- Use job advertisements to find the right keywords and phrases.
- Be prepared to change the job title in your profile.
- Customise your profile for every job application.
- Give the recruiters what they are looking for.

Identifying your key skills and experience

Assuming the recruiter is sufficiently impressed with your profile, they will now start checking your CV in a little more detail.

In most job advertisements and job specifications you will find a list of 'essential skills and experience' for the job. If the job advertisement doesn't set out the requirements clearly then call the recruiter and ask for more information. Very often the recruiter will be able to provide you with a more detailed job specification from the employer or alternatively they will be able to tell you the key requirements for the job. These might be a combination of qualifications, skills, experience and personal attributes.

Have a look at this job advertisement for a finance director.

Essential skills and experience

- A qualified accountant, graduate calibre with an outstanding track record of financial leadership, ideally with experience gained within a large, complex organisation within the mobile communications sector.

- Strategic, innovative and entrepreneurial, able to identify and manage the risk of new commercial opportunities.

- A first-class negotiator with strong communication and analytical skills; sound judgement and an engaging and collaborative personal style.

We can start off with a profile that contains sufficient information to attract the recruiter's attention.

Versatile senior finance director with 10 years' experience in senior financial leadership. A qualified accountant with excellent experience in strategic management and with a proven ability to identify and manage risk. Seeking a challenging new role in the field of mobile telecommunications.

Having read the profile the recruiter will be looking for further evidence of the skills, qualifications and experience specified in the advertisement. Candidates who don't have the 'essential skills and experience' will go straight into the 'no' pile. It is sometimes the case that candidates *do* have the required experience but it is hidden away on page 10 of their CV. It is extremely unlikely that the recruiter will have time to search the CV to find that information. The recruiter probably has a couple of hours to find two or three strong candidates to put forward to the client. So it's your task to make sure that the recruiter can clearly see evidence of those key skills, qualifications and personal attributes as quickly and as easily as possible.

Key items that the recruiter will be searching for based on the advertisement for the finance director role:

- qualified accountant/graduate calibre
- senior financial leadership experience
- experience in a large, complex organisation
- strategic
- innovative/entrepreneurial
- manages risk of commercial opportunities
- negotiation skills
- strong communication skills
- analytical
- sound judgement
- experience in the mobile telecommunications sector.

Let's now develop a list of key skills, qualifications and experience that can sit directly below your profile and within the first screen of your CV. Remember, your aim is to make your CV as attractive as possible to the recruiter for this particular job. Different job advertisements will place a different emphasis on other aspects of your skill set.

Of course, you must not include skills and experience that you do not have or personal attributes that you cannot support at interview!

For example, if you have never 'managed the risk of new commercial opportunities' then clearly you cannot state that you have done so in your CV. Remember also that this example is given for a finance director but the principle of matching the content of your CV to the exact requirements as set out in the job advertisement can be applied to any job, whether it's for a sales director or an airline pilot.

We are looking for a way to show that you have all the skills, qualifications and experience specified in the job advertisement. There are two ways that you can do this. One way is to list the key skills that you have identified in a simple table directly under your profile. We now have the important information that will sell you to a recruiter clearly visible at the top of page one of your CV.

Richard Green

128 Reading Lane, Reading, Berkshire RG90 4XX,
United Kingdom
Telephone: 01234 567891
Email: richard.green@email.com

Versatile senior finance director with 10 years' experience in senior financial leadership. A qualified accountant with excellent experience in strategic management and with a proven ability to identify and manage risk. Seeking a challenging new role in the field of mobile telecommunications.

KEY SKILLS AND EXPERIENCE

Qualified accountant	Good communication skills
Financial leadership experience	Analytical
Strategic management	Sound judgement
Innovative/entrepreneurial	Experience of cost control
Risk management skills	Mobile telecommunication
Good negotiation skills	Degree in economics

That list certainly meets most of the requirements set out in the job advertisement for the finance director. This type of list is an extremely effective way of highlighting your key skills that are relevant for a particular role. They enable the recruiter to simply tick off the required skills and qualifications. When a recruiter is very busy and pressed for time they will welcome the opportunity to be able to quickly match you to the job and place your CV in their 'yes' pile for further review. For the majority of jobs this is the most effective way to customise your CV for a particular role. Check the job advertisement or job specification, match the requirements to your own background and then list your relevant skills, qualifications and experience in two columns under your profile. We'll look at more examples of this technique later in this chapter.

TOTAL JOB SEARCH TIP

Customise your CV by listing your matching skills, qualifications and experience.

There is another way to present your key skills and experience which is more suited to the CVs of job hunters who may have more qualifications and experience than candidates at the beginning of their career or with just a few years' experience. If you are at this level then you can use short **competency statements** that provide more detailed information relating to the key skills and experience required for a particular role. My own experience when recruiting more experienced candidates is that I want to see a little more evidence of what a candidate has to offer. Faced with a pool of experienced and well qualified candidates it's this extra information that may just make the difference between a candidate being shortlisted or not. It's a personal decision and you should use the format that works best for you. Remember that your objective is to set out the specific skills, qualifications and experience that match you to the job and to make that information as accessible as possible for the recruiter.

Here are some examples of suitable competency statements for the finance director role.

KEY SKILLS AND EXPERIENCE

Qualified accountant. A member of the Institute of Chartered Accountants in England and Wales. Substantial senior-level experience of managing finance in a large, complex organisation.

Financial leadership. Takes full responsibility for financial management and control of operations. Provides leadership in planning, accounting and budgeting. Fully capable of working in partnership with the board of directors to ensure delivery of financial targets.

Strategic management. Provides strategic leadership in an advisory/consultative role in all financial decision-making and assists with formulating and executing innovative and effective business strategies.

Leadership. Expertise in managing high-performing teams of finance professionals. Ensures effective performance management of the teams via meaningful appraisals, goal-setting, feedback and coaching.

Commercial focus. An entrepreneurial flair and a strong commercial awareness. Identifies opportunities for increased revenues. Offers specialist financial advice to the board of directors to ensure optimal business decision-making.

Risk management. Creates economic value by using financial instruments to manage exposure to risk. Experience of identifying and measuring risk and developing effective plans to either mitigate or eliminate exposure to commercial or financial risk.

Communication. Proven ability to interact at every level within an organisation and to engage effectively with colleagues, customers and senior management in a collaborative and friendly manner.

Cost control. Real expertise in implementing effective cost control initiatives. Manages all the commercial aspects of day-to-day operations including negotiation of agreements with third party suppliers and vendors to secure the most cost-effective business services.

Now let's see how that information might look to a recruiter viewing the CV on the first screen of a computer.

Richard Green

128 Reading Lane, Reading, Berkshire RG90 4XX,
United Kingdom
Telephone: 01234 567891
Email: richard.green@email.com

Versatile senior finance director with 10 years' experience in senior financial leadership. A qualified accountant with excellent experience in strategic management and with a proven ability to identify and manage risk. A forward-thinking individual offering significant cross-functional expertise and a proven ability to stimulate business improvement. Seeking a challenging new role in mobile telecommunications.

KEY SKILLS AND EXPERIENCE

Qualified chartered accountant. A member of the Institute of Chartered Accountants in England and Wales. Substantial senior-level experience of managing finance in a large, complex organisation.	**Financial leadership.** Takes full responsibility for financial management and control of operations. Provides leadership in planning, accounting and budgeting. Fully capable of working in partnership with the board of directors to ensure delivery of financial targets.
Strategic management. Provides strategic leadership in an advisory/consultative role in all financial decision-making and assists with formulating and executing innovative and effective business strategies.	**Risk management.** Creates economic value by using financial instruments to manage exposure to risk. Experience of identifying and measuring risk and developing effective plans to either mitigate or eliminate exposure to commercial or financial risk.
Leadership. Expertise in managing high-performing teams of finance professionals. Ensures effective performance management of teams via meaningful appraisals and goal-setting.	**Communication.** Proven ability to interact at every level within an organisation and to engage effectively with colleagues, customers and senior management in a collaborative and friendly manner.
Commercial focus. An entrepreneurial flair and a strong commercial awareness. Identifies opportunities for increased revenues. Offers specialist financial advice to the board of directors to ensure optimal business decision-making.	**Cost control.** Real expertise in implementing effective cost control initiatives. Manages all the commercial aspects of day-to-day operations including negotiation of agreements with third party suppliers and vendors to secure the most cost-effective business services.

Note that all of the information required to qualify Richard Green is visible immediately in the first screen. The recruiter does not need to scroll down to see that this candidate *does* have the required skills, experience and qualifications for the job. The recruiter can also see that there is some evidence to support the statements.

How do I write my own competency statements?

Here are some further examples of short competency statements that are commonly required for management jobs. You can adapt them to match your own professional background.

Strategic management. Proven ability to make a positive medium and long-term impact by drawing up coherent strategic plans, sometimes based on incomplete or ambiguous information. Developing the corporate vision.

Leadership. Managing and motivating high-performing multi-disciplined teams. Ensuring effective performance management of the teams via meaningful goal-setting, feedback and coaching.

Budget management. Responsible for project budgets of up to $12 million. Effective management of third party resources and external vendors and suppliers.

Customer relationship management. A focus on managing key client relationships and the negotiation of contracts. Further responsibility for quickly establishing trusting client relationships and assuring the fulfilment of contractual obligations.

Project management. Hands-on experience of managing the full life cycle of projects. A qualified project management professional (PMP).

Commercial focus. An entrepreneurial flair and a strong commercial awareness. Identifying opportunities for increased revenues. Offering specialist financial advice to ensure optimal business decision-making.

Business change. Real expertise in initiating fundamental change relating to both the market and operating model of a number of large, complex organisations. Managing change in order to respond rapidly to market dynamics.

Organisational development. Provides expertise in support of reorganisation, restructure and business growth in line with the strategic needs of the business.

Networking. Selects key business partners and establishes strategic alliances with the objective of growing the business and identifying new business opportunities leading to increased revenues.

Business development. Works alongside the business development teams to identify new opportunities and develops and manages a network of senior-level relationships with customers and potential customers.

Communication. Strong communication skills. Proven ability to interact at every level within an organisation and to communicate effectively with both financial and non-financial managers.

Motivated. A highly motivated individual with excellent analytical and problem-solving skills and a proven ability to deliver against key business metrics.

TOTAL JOB SEARCH TIP

For more senior roles use short competency statements in your CV.

Beware of very general statements like 'reliable' or 'enthusiastic'. These are essentially meaningless unless they are supported by some proper evidence of how these attributes would be relevant to the employer.

Your career achievements

The next key area that interests recruiters is your career achievements: in other words, *further* evidence that you have specific work experience that is relevant to the employer's needs and would directly benefit their business.

As one leading recruiter recently stated:

'I don't just want a job description; I want to know what the candidate achieved and how it made a difference to the employer.'

Very typically on CVs I find statements that simply describe the duties and responsibilities of an individual. Many people simply take the words from their job descriptions and paste them into their CV.

For example, here's a rather bland extract from the CV of a business development manager.

Managed business development team for North East Region.

Now let's rewrite that bulleted phrase so that we can see what was actually achieved in that role and how it made a difference to the employer.

Managed the North East Region Business Development Team. Tasked with achieving challenging sales targets; provided formal training and coaching and inspired and motivated the team to achieve 120% of sales targets in 3 consecutive years.

Now that's impressive! As an employer I'd certainly want to speak to a candidate who could potentially replicate that success in my business.

Identifying and describing your achievements

Listing your career achievements is a key element of a good CV. This is critically important and your CV will stand out if you make the effort to write up your achievements effectively. We're interested in achievements that are:

- recent
- relevant
- rare
- personal (achievements about you).

Recent. Because something that you did 10 years ago is almost certainly not going to reflect your capabilities today.

Relevant. We need to select achievements that will be relevant to our potential employer. In the job advertisement for the finance director there was a requirement to 'identify and manage risk'. Therefore a strong achievement relating to risk reduction would be highly relevant to that particular employer.

Rare. Ideally your achievements should be special and related to you and your unique skills. Try to think of achievements that set you apart from all the other candidates competing for the job. In this context something unusual, special or innovative will definitely catch the employer's attention.

Personal. You should avoid the use of 'we'. Remember that this CV document is about *you* and *your* achievements. A CV is not the place to be modest! Remember, the recruiter wants to know about your achievements and what you did to make a difference for your employer.

There is a simple technique that will enable you to write about your achievements effectively.

Using STAR to describe your achievements

Use the **STAR** acronym to structure your achievements.

- Situation
- Task
- Action
- Result

Using the STAR format to describe your achievements is a very powerful technique. It ensures that the description of your achievement is well structured and, most importantly, it highlights what you actually did (the action) and the strong positive result that you achieved for your employer.

Let's see how we could use the STAR structure to write up some of Richard Green's experiences as achievements in his CV.

Situation

When Richard started his last job as finance director he found that many of the company's supplier agreements for company vehicles, mobile phones and IT service management had not been reviewed for a number of years.

Task

Richard set himself the task of achieving a substantial saving on each of the supplier agreements.

Action

Richard contacted all of the suppliers and asked them to re-tender for the business. He also contacted a number of alternative suppliers for each of the services. He held a competitive tender process. He evaluated all of the proposals and then awarded new contracts.

Result

Richard was able to achieve average savings of 25% on the current charges and in some cases actually to improve the level of service provided.

That achievement will definitely be relevant and will be of considerable interest to the employer advertising for a new finance director.

We can now write up this achievement in Richard's CV using the STAR format.

The company's supplier agreements had not been reviewed for a number of years. Tasked with reducing costs on existing supplier agreements. Set up a competitive tender with a number of suppliers to provide core services including mobile telephony, IT service management and vehicle leasing. Evaluated supplier proposals and negotiated new contracts resulting in average cost savings of 25% accompanied by significantly improved levels of service.

Note how the STAR format helps to structure the achievement and highlights the specific benefit – the result that would impress a potential employer.

When describing your experience, it is best to do so using strong **action words**. These words can appear in the descriptions of your career achievements or past employment sections. They detail the action you undertook to achieve a task and the results achieved by your actions. For example, when describing your duties in a past position you might say you:

- **set up** a competitive tender
- **organised** a campaign
- **managed** a project
- **liaised** with clients
- **identified** new business opportunities
- **established** new client contacts.

Try to write up at least 10 of your achievements using the STAR model. You should ideally have no more than four to five achievements in your CV. However, be prepared to be flexible and change the wording of the achievements to ensure that they are relevant to the needs of your potential employer. Remember you can identify those needs by referring to the job advertisement or to the job specification. In addition, you can undertake some further research either by asking the recruiter directly or by checking for further information about your potential employer in the press or on the internet.

WRITE ABOUT YOUR OWN ACHIEVEMENTS USING THE STAR FORMAT

1.
_____
_____
_____
_____

2.
_____
_____
_____
_____

3.
_____
_____
_____
_____

4.
_____
_____
_____
_____

5.
_____
_____
_____
_____

Customising your achievements

The two case studies below illustrate that undertaking some thorough research and customising your achievements for a specific role can pay dividends.

CASE STUDY: SALES MANAGER

Sarah wanted to respond to an advertisement for a sales manager role with a paper manufacturer. The job advertisement simply stated a requirement for 'previous team management experience'. Sarah took the initiative and first called the recruiter handling the vacancy to try and find out a little more about what the employer was actually looking for. The recruiter was able to confirm that at previous interviews the company had focused on the candidates' experience of 'turning around' and motivating a poorly performing sales team. Furthermore, it appeared that the previous incumbent in the job had been dismissed because of irregularities in the sales figures and expenses. Clearly the sales team was somewhat demoralised and needed a new manager to re-motivate them and put them back on track. As it happened, Sarah *did* have previous experience of inspiring and re-motivating a sales team. She then added an achievement to her CV which specifically described this scenario and the actions that she took to revitalise the team and dramatically improve their sales performance. Not surprisingly this was exactly what the employer was looking for and Sarah was subsequently offered the job.

Look at Sarah's customised achievement as written on her CV.

As the newly appointed Sales Manager at Penmore Communications, tasked with turning around a sales team with a history of poor performance against sales targets. Instigated regular team meetings, formal and informal coaching sessions and accompanied individual team members on sales calls. Set personal action plans with clearly defined performance targets. Within 6 months we had a real team spirit and sales figures had improved by 25%.

CASE STUDY: PROJECT MANAGER

Michael wanted to apply for a role as a project manager. He undertook some research and noted from the employer's website and from reports in the press that the company was proposing to merge a large number of regional offices into a single head office. Michael had extensive experience of managing office moves and therefore introduced an achievement in his CV that related to a recent, very large-scale office relocation that had been completed successfully and with minimal disruption to the business. This experience was clearly very relevant to the employer and Michael was offered the job.

Look at Michael's customised achievement.

As the Project and Facilities Manager at Danforth Construction, I was tasked with managing a major project to relocate 100 staff and associated IT systems from three different locations to a new headquarters building. Worked closely with the IT Manager and a number of external contractors to manage the move. The relocation project was successfully accomplished over a single weekend with zero defects and minimal disruption to the business.

In both instances the specific experience was not mentioned in either the job advertisement or the job specification and only came to light when the candidates undertook some further research prior to sending off their CVs.

Remember that job advertisements are often rather generic and companies will not necessarily divulge any problems they might have in a public advertisement. Digging a little deeper is always worthwhile. It also illustrates the importance of keeping the CV document flexible and taking the trouble to customise each job application.

TOTAL JOB SEARCH TIP

Customise your achievements for each role.

Your career history

Moving on from the career achievements section we now come to the section of the CV covering your **career history**. Always start with the most recent role first and begin by clearly stating the dates that you worked for that particular employer and your **job title**. Many organisations use internal job titles that contain company jargon or acronyms that would be clearly understood within that organisation but would be unrecognisable or confusing to outsiders. You may wish to consider changing the job title to more closely match the job that you are applying for or putting the 'real world' job title in brackets after your internal job title. There is nothing wrong with this practice providing you don't promote yourself to a much more senior position!

Some examples might include the following.

Internal job title	Real world job title
Client Relationship Manager	Sales Manager
ERP Delivery Specialist	IT Project Manager
Media Fulfilment Officer	Web Manager

The issue of job titles has become a real problem in recruitment and many recruiters will have had experience of reading through a CV and struggling to understand what exactly someone actually does. So try to use plain English and, where appropriate, try to closely match the job title that is actually used in the job advertisement.

If you work in administration and you manage a team you are an '**administration manager**' regardless of your internal job title.

The issue of job titles can also cause problems from another perspective. Some employers (particularly those with a US connection) very freely use the title 'vice president' for roles which in other parts of the world might be considered middle management roles.

If your CV states that you are '**vice president media relations**' when your role more closely matches that of a **PR manager** then you may well find yourself being sidelined because you are considered too senior for a particular job.

While it may be nice to have the VP in your job title it could actually have a negative impact on your job search. Assuming that you are applying for a PR manager job then you should consider changing it.

So for each role you can now record your time with a particular organisation as follows.

May 2007 – Present
Production Manager
Paper Company Ltd
Global supplier of paper products employing 10,000 people and with an annual turnover of £1.2 billion.

Note the brief description of the company under the company name so that recruiters know something about the employer.

Against each job you should now record between five and 10 bullets highlighting your key achievements during your time there. A very good test to apply to each bullet is to ask the question '**So what?**' after each statement.

Take the following rather dull bullets:

- led a team of 20 sales staff
- managed the office relocation project
- devised the staff incentive scheme.

The 'So what?' test

By applying the 'So what?' test you can transform these dull statements into bullet points that will be infinitely more appealing to recruiters and employers.

Note that in each case we have added a **result** to the original statement. How would you respond if a recruiter or interviewer said 'So what?' after each statement in your CV? Try to think carefully about what positive things happened after you did something in your job. Of course, you must not exaggerate and you must be able to back up any statements with hard evidence. It doesn't matter if you don't have dramatic successes, just focus on the results of your efforts so that the employer can see clearly what you could offer to their business. Again, it's important to ensure that the experience you offer is relevant to the job you are applying for. Don't spend whole pages writing about your employer's new telephony system or their successful award of ISO 9000 accreditation unless this has some relevance to the job you are applying for.

Rather than using the full STAR acronym to describe your work experience, use the simplified **action** and **result** model. Look at the following example.

Action	Result
Led an award-winning team	that exceeded all performance targets
Successfully managed a large and complex office relocation	with minimal disruption to the business
Devised an enhanced staff incentive scheme	that dramatically reduced staff turnover

As you work back through your career you may find that your CV is becoming too long. The ideal CV length is two or three pages. If you believe that your CV is going to be much longer then you should consider simply recording the dates, employer name and your title for jobs that you did more than 10 years ago. Generally employers are going to be more interested in your recent experience as most of us have progressed in our careers.

Recording your early career

You could use the following format to record jobs that you undertook more than 10 years ago.

EARLY CAREER

May 1997 – Aug 2000	Ericsson	Head of Finance
Jan 1994 – April 1997	Philips	Accountant
Oct 1990 – Dec 1993	IBM	Intern

Although there are no details of your work at those times there is still a significant amount of information. The eagle-eyed HR manager will be looking for any gaps in your career history and this table shows that you were fully employed prior to 2000 and that you were able to move from job to job without any breaks in your employment. Furthermore, it is also clear that during this period you worked for prestigious blue-chip employers and that you made rapid progress from the position of intern to head of finance in only 10 years. Quite an achievement! We'll be looking at how to deal with periods of unemployment later in this chapter (see page 72).

Your professional qualifications and education

Following on from your career history you can detail any professional qualifications and training as well as your education. Unless you are a recent school leaver or recent graduate you should not include details of your school exams (e.g. GCSEs in the UK). This section of your CV might now look like this.

EDUCATION AND PROFESSIONAL QUALIFICATIONS	
2000	MBA – London Business School
1998	Chartered Accountant (FCCA)
1994	BSc Economics (2:i) Exeter University

Additional information

A final section of your CV could include some additional information not covered so far.

ADDITIONAL INFORMATION	
Nationality:	British
Languages:	Native English, fluent French and Spanish
Interests:	Football, golf and sailing
References:	Available on request

You can see the completed CV on the following two pages. Although this example is provided for a finance director the same format will be effective for any role. You will find further examples of CVs in different job categories and at different experience levels later in this chapter.

Richard Green

128 Reading Lane, Reading, Berkshire RG90 4XX, United Kingdom
Telephone 01234 567891
Email: richard.green@email.com

Versatile senior finance director with 10 years' experience in senior financial leadership. A qualified accountant with excellent experience in strategic management and with a proven ability to identify and manage risk. A forward-thinking individual offering significant cross-functional management expertise and a proven ability to stimulate business improvement. Seeking a challenging new role in the field of mobile telecommunications.

KEY SKILLS AND EXPERIENCE

Qualified chartered accountant. A member of the Institute of Chartered Accountants in England and Wales. Substantial senior-level experience of managing finance in a large, complex organisation.	**Financial leadership.** Takes full responsibility for financial management and control of operations. Provides leadership in planning, accounting and budgeting. Fully capable of working in partnership with the board of directors to ensure delivery of financial targets.
Strategic management. Provides strategic leadership in an advisory/consultative role in all financial decision-making and assists with formulating and executing innovative and effective business strategies.	**Risk management.** Creates economic value by using financial instruments to manage exposure to risk. Experience of identifying and measuring risk and developing effective plans to either mitigate or eliminate exposure to commercial or financial risk.
Leadership. Expertise in managing high-performing teams of finance professionals. Ensures effective performance management of the teams via meaningful appraisals, goal-setting and feedback.	**Communication.** Proven ability to interact at every level within an organisation and to engage effectively with colleagues in a collaborative and friendly manner. Significant experience of presenting and reporting at board level.
Commercial focus. An entrepreneurial flair and a strong commercial awareness. Identifies opportunities for increased revenues. Offers specialist financial advice to the board of directors.	**Cost control.** Real expertise in implementing effective cost control initiatives. Manages all the commercial aspects of day-to-day operations including negotiation of supplier agreements. Achieved significant cost savings.

SELECTED CAREER ACHIEVEMENTS

- Identified an opportunity to reduce costs on existing supplier agreements. Set up a competitive tender with a number of suppliers to provide core services including mobile telephony, IT service management and vehicle leasing. Evaluated supplier proposals and negotiated new contracts resulting in average cost savings of 25% accompanied by significantly improved levels of service.
- Following an in-depth review, made the decision to outsource the finance function in some countries and expanded the roles of some of the UK team to focus on European operations. Reduced headcount within the European finance team from 21 to 11 people. As a result, significantly improved management information across the whole business.
- Reviewed the medium-term strategic goals for the business. Developed a financial model to enable priorities and the framework to achieve these goals. This led to the identification and acquisition of a complementary business together with the establishment of operations in Australia. Managed the extension of and reduction in the cost of off-shoring of development roles.

EMPLOYMENT HISTORY

May 2007 – Present
Finance Director
Paper Company Ltd
Global supplier of paper products employing 10,000 people and with an annual turnover of £1.2 billion.
- Built strong relationships with senior stakeholders and developed working relationships with clients.
- Supported the business in the preparation of budgets and forecasts.
- Reduced operating costs by 25% following a review of existing service agreements.
- Delivered solid monthly and annual reporting to provide accurate financial/management information.
- Undertook a succesful change management project following the acquisition of another business.
- Demonstrated good team-building skills and increased the finance team from 10 to 20 staff.

May 2004 – April 2007
Assistant Finance Director
Proctor Company Ltd
Leading global financial services business with a turnover of £500 million.
- Provided full financial and commercial support to the finance director.
- Ensured the timely delivery of accurate and insightful management accounts.
- Worked with the finance director to deliver the annual budget and 5-year financial plan.
- Ensured that appropriate financial controls were in place to control expenditure.
- Reviewed operational and capital expenditure.
- Reduced operating costs by 10% on a budget of £90 million.
- Reduced headcount within the finance team while maintaining accounting standards.

April 2000 – May 2004
Assistant Finance Director
Basking Company Ltd
Global business and technology services company.
- Delivered accurate monthly, quarterly and annual reports.
- Developed and maintained all aspects of the internal control environment.
- Prepared monthly and annual rolling budgets.
- Carried out cash planning with currency control (hedges, bank collections).
- Provided treasury guidance, payment and Forex control.

1994 – 1999
Graduate Trainee
Smith Hodgkinson and Partners
Chartered accountants.
- Set up and maintained financial data on IT systems.
- Worked on site with clients as part of the auditing team.
- Provided support to the auditing teams.
- Studied for accountancy exams on a day-release basis.

EDUCATION AND PROFESSIONAL QUALIFICATIONS

2000	MBA – London Business School
1998	Chartered Accountant (ICAEW)
1994	BSc Economics (2:i) Exeter University

ADDITIONAL INFORMATION

Nationality:	British
Languages:	Native English, fluent French and Spanish
Interests:	Football, golf and sailing
References:	Available on request

You do not need to include the names and contact details of your referees in your CV. You can supply details of your referees at the job offer stage. Although having a written testimonial can be useful, most employers will still want to contact your referees directly either by phone or in writing. At the appropriate time it would be advisable to contact your referees and confirm that they are still able to provide you with a reference. At the same time you could give them some brief details of the job you are being considered for and the particular experience or skills that the employer is looking for. This way your referees will be well prepared when your future employer calls.

Using keywords in your CV

If you thought recruiting was just about people, you may be surprised to learn that a lot of recruiting is actually handled by computers. When you apply for a job on an internet job site or with a recruitment agency or when you email a speculative CV to a company it's important to understand *how* it is going to be read. As you write your CV you may imagine that it will be printed and then carefully read and reviewed by a potential employer. While this is certainly sometimes the case, the more likely scenario is that your CV will have been stored on a recruitment agency database or internet job site and will be read on a computer screen. I have to say that from personal experience it is very easy to review up to 50 CVs in less than 10 minutes. Recruiters routinely flick through large numbers of CVs making snap judgements on the suitability of individual candidates in less than 10 seconds. The message is very clear. Your CV needs to be written in a format that enables the recruiter to see the key information, including keywords that sell you and match you to a particular role, in the very first screen of information, i.e. the top half of page one of your CV.

Many recruiters will have found your CV by way of a keyword search. That is to say they will take the keywords from a job specification and search CVs from the agency database and the internet job sites for likely candidates who most closely match their profile of the ideal candidate for a particular role.

Look at this extract from a recent job advertisement.

> **Looking for an experienced factory manager with a strong manufacturing background in the ceramics industry.**

A typical recruiter's search might look like this:

'Factory manager' AND ceramics AND manufacturing.

This search will pull up all the CVs on the database that contain those keywords and phrases. Now you can't blame the recruiter for using those particular words in the search, after all that's what the client is asking for, but if your CV states that you are a production manager for sanitaryware and tiles without mentioning the words **manufacturing** or **ceramics** then your CV may not be found. You need to be aware of *all* the keywords that are most likely to be searched for a particular kind of job.

Find keywords in job advertisements

Many people will be aware of the phrase 'search engine optimisation' (SEO), which involves placing the right keywords throughout a web page. This process generally begins with web designers researching what keywords are used by people when searching for particular items or topics on the internet using a search engine such as Google.

In exactly the same way you must try to identify the keywords and phrases that recruiters will be searching for to find people like you. The easiest way to find out what these words are is to continually review advertisements (on the internet or in the press) for jobs that you would like to apply for. Start listing all of the words and phrases that seem to appear again and again in those advertisements. Make sure that you then include the appropriate keywords and phrases in your CV. This will ensure that your CV is found by recruiters when they are searching for suitable candidates.

Here are some extracts from three job advertisements for sales managers. Note the keywords and phrases that are used in each of the advertisements.

> Excellent communication and negotiation skills. Strong organisational and persuasion skills. A good team player with a strong work ethic.

> Proven track record of finding new named accounts and closing deals of £100k+. Experienced at planning marketing campaigns and events.

> Day-to-day management of a team of travel consultants and be motivating, target driven and a natural leader.

From these advertisements we can extract several useful keywords and phrases that will often appear in sales manager job advertisements.

For example:

- excellent communication skills
- negotiation skills
- strong organisational skills
- persuasion skills
- team player
- finding new accounts
- closing deals
- planning marketing campaigns
- motivating
- target driven.

Be flexible and keep reviewing job advertisements to make sure that you have the right keywords in your CV.

Once your CV has been found, you need to be sure that it stands out. Place those keywords prominently in the **key skills and experience** and **career achievements** sections of your CV and consider placing the most relevant in bold type. That way the recruiter just can't miss them!

It is extremely important that your CV clearly states all of your skills and abilities to maximise its potential for recognition by the computer search. You may even want to tailor keywords in your CV each time you submit it for a different role. When tailoring your keywords, be sure to include words relating to your skills, your experience, the sector and the specific role.

TOTAL JOB SEARCH TIP

Use the right keywords in your CV.

Job titles as keywords

Including the titles of your past jobs and of roles you're looking for is effective in making your CV stand out in relevant computer searches. These titles can be included in the employment history section of your CV and in the professional profile paragraph respectively. As previously stated, recruiters are usually focused on a particular job title when engaged in a search. Make sure that you use job titles that closely match the job that you are applying for. Most recruiters will have come across (by chance!) the CVs of candidates who are exactly right for a particular job but do not have any of the right keywords in their CV. Of course, the best recruiters will look carefully at every CV that is sent to them and, if they are experienced, have the skills and industry knowledge to recognise that a 'customer satisfaction manager', might be the ideal candidate for the position of 'customer relationship manager', but rather than making the recruiter's job more difficult we are in the business of making it easier.

If you are applying for the position of customer relationship manager and you have all of the required skills and experience requested in the job advertisement then consider using that job title in your application. If you don't then you risk being left out of searches or not being shortlisted for interview.

But please remember, don't change your job title unless it accurately represents what you actually do and you can back it up with real experience of fulfilling that type of role.

CVs for different job categories and levels of experience

On the following pages we'll look at CVs for different job categories and for job hunters at different stages of their careers.

The graduate CV

One very important category is the recent graduate CV. The obvious disadvantage for recent graduates is that they just don't have much work experience. Nevertheless, when applying for that first job, employers *do* still want to see a CV. So as a recent graduate what should you include?

Include full details of your degree and include your degree classification. As you are just setting out on your career it will also be helpful to include some details of your performance at school: details of your A level results and how many GCSEs you have, particularly if they are relevant to the job you are applying for. Also include any work experience you had during your degree course. Describe the job and ensure your line manager will be prepared to provide a reference if requested. If you don't have degree-related work experience but have worked as a part-time shop assistant, barman or waitress then do include this work and emphasise what you feel you learnt from this (e.g. team-working, sales skills, dealing with customers). If you were active in any extracurricular activities such as organising sporting or social events be sure to include these as well. Did you have a gap year? Where did you go? What did you do? What did you learn?

In the absence of any career achievements, what about your personal achievements? (You could include Duke of Edinburgh's Award, music grades, public speaking, charity runs and so on.) Generally, recruiters will not expect more than a one-page CV from a recent graduate. But the basic format can still include the same sections as outlined earlier in this chapter.

PROFILE
KEY SKILLS AND EXPERIENCE
SELECTED ACHIEVEMENTS
WORK EXPERIENCE
EDUCATION
ADDITIONAL INFORMATION

An example CV for a recent graduate

Richard Stark

48 Northgate Road, London N1 3JH
Telephone: 01234 567891
Email: richardstark@anymail.com

PROFILE

A graduate in Human Resources Management with 12 months' experience of both administration and management in a work placement with a blue-chip employer in the defence sector. A proven ability to work effectively in a commercial environment and capable of quickly learning new skills. Available now for a challenging HR role with a large or small organisation.

KEY SKILLS AND EXPERIENCE

HR work experience	Organised and efficient administration
Strong commercial awareness	Excellent communication skills
Excellent analytical/problem-solving skills	Strong IT skills including Microsoft Office
Committed team player	BSc in HR Management from the University of Bath

SELECTED ACHIEVEMENTS

- Organised a charity fundraising dinner for Cancer Research
- Raised £500 from a charity skydive
- Captained the university hockey team
- Ran the London Marathon in 2011
- Achieved Duke of Edinburgh's Gold Award

WORK EXPERIENCE

July 2009 – July 2010
HR Administrator
March Aviation (12-month work placement)

- Assisted in the development of HR policies for the UK business.
- Supported the HR manager with managing disciplinary and grievance procedures.
- Assisted with the recruitment of staff.
- Presented the company induction to new starters.
- Administered HR-related documentation including employment contracts.
- Acted as the first point of contact for employee enquiries.
- Managed the employee information system and ensured that it was accurate and up to date.

EDUCATION

Sep 2007 – July 2011	University of Bath
	BSc (Hons) Human Resource Management – 2:i
Sep 2000 – July 2007	Bath High School
	GCSE: 8 subjects including Maths and English
	A levels: English, Geography and French

IT SKILLS

Microsoft Office – Word, Excel and PowerPoint

ADDITIONAL INFORMATION

Nationality:	British
Interests:	Running, tennis, sailing and charity fundraising
References:	Available on request

An example CV for an 'early career' role in financial services

Compare Richard Green's CV as a finance director (see page 56) and this CV from earlier in his career. Note the shorter competency statements and the inclusion of one-line career achievements that reflect his relative lack of experience. Note also that at this early stage in his career he has also included his excellent academic results from school, which reinforce his language abilities and his suitability for a role with an international dimension.

Richard Green

128 Reading Lane, Reading, Berkshire RG90 4XX,
United Kingdom
Telephone: 01234 567891
Email: richard.green@email.com

Versatile financial accountant with 5 years' experience in financial services. A qualified chartered accountant with excellent experience in producing monthly financial reports and year-end financial accounts. A proven history of performing well under pressure and with excellent technical and analytical skills using Excel and Sage. Seeking a challenging new role with an international dimension where I can make use of my fluent French and Spanish.

KEY SKILLS AND EXPERIENCE

BSc in Economics (2:i)	Preparation of daily profit and loss accounts
Qualified chartered accountant (ICAEW)	Preparation of monthly financial reports
5 years' work experience	Assisting in the production of year-end financial accounts
Technical expertise with Sage and Excel	Dealing with customers in the UK and Europe
Financial process improvement	Fluent French and Spanish

SELECTED CAREER ACHIEVEMENTS

- Passed all final exams as a chartered accountant at the first attempt.
- Successfully upgraded the Sage accounting system at Smith Hodgkinson and Partners.
- Undertook a project to optimise the process for managing the completion of clients' year-end financial accounts.
- Dealt with a number of clients based in Europe and identified and secured additional European business.
- Received a letter of commendation from the European Head of Practice following a cost-reduction initiative.

EMPLOYMENT HISTORY

1994 – Present

Graduate Trainee

Smith Hodgkinson and Partners

Chartered accountants.

- Set up and maintained financial data and created a more efficient and robust IT system.
- Worked on site with clients in both the UK and Europe as part of the inernational auditing team.
- Provided support to the auditing teams including working with clients in both French and Spanish.
- Studied for accountancy exams on a day-release basis and achieved a first-time pass in all subjects.

EDUCATION AND PROFESSIONAL QUALIFICATIONS

1998	Chartered Accountant (ICAEW)
1994	BSc Economics (2:i) Exeter University
1990	Graduated from Reading High School with A grades in Maths, French and Spanish

ADDITIONAL INFORMATION

Nationality:	British
Languages:	Native English, fluent French and Spanish
Interests:	Football, golf and sailing
References:	Available on request

Example CV extract for a job in IT

If you work in IT then the key skills and experience required will almost certainly relate to your expertise in a particular technology. In IT each of the technical skills becomes an important searchable keyword. My advice would be to place your key technical skills at the top of your CV and directly under your profile where they can be seen easily by the recruiter. Here's an example of a more technical CV that still uses the same basic format described earlier in this chapter.

Khalid Shah MSc

83 Long Eaton Drive, Southmead, Surrey GU27 3LN
Tel: 01234 567891
Email: khalid.shah@email.com

Skilled enterprise architect with more than 5 years' experience of resolving complex business problems with innovative enterprise solutions. Strong knowledge of structured analysis and design techniques including process and data-modelling such as expertise in IDEF, BPMN, UML and Archimate. Now looking for a challenging new contract role in the investment banking sector.

KEY SKILLS AND EXPERIENCE

Enterprise architecture	Process methodologies	Software development
• Business/IT alignment	• Frameworks (ITIL, CMMI)	• Software processes (Agile, RUP, XP, Scrum)
• IT transformation	• Security and compliance (FISMA, NIST 800 pubs)	• Open source
• Enterprise modernisation	• Project assessment and remediation	• AJAX
• Cloud computing	• Architecture evaluation (SEI ATAM)	• Java
• Social media, Web 2.0	• PRINCE2	• VBA Excel
• SOA, web services	• Waterfall	• VB, .NET
• Frameworks (TOGAF, IDEF)	• Agile	• C++, C#
• BPMN, UML	• SCRUM	

Example CV extract for a senior role in education

Rachel Arnold

32 Fontwell Drive, East Slendon, Wiltshire WA56 3TY
Telephone: 01234 567891
Email: rachel.arnold@email.com

Head teacher with over 10 years' experience in developing strategies to drive academic improvement at all levels of educational development. A proven ability to lead schools and other educational establishments and to create a nurturing and safe school environment dedicated to achieving excellence. Now seeking a challenging new role in educational leadership in either the UK or abroad.

KEY SKILLS AND EXPERIENCE

Qualified teacher. A fully qualified teacher with a BA from the University of Bangor and a postgraduate MSc in Education and Training Management from the University of Portsmouth.	**Curriculum development.** Able to lead and inspire curriculum development across the school. Enthusiastic about creativity in the curriculum and committed to excellence in all aspects of teaching and learning.
Leadership. A highly motivational leader and a first-class school manager with excellent interpersonal skills.	**Inclusive.** Fully committed to maintaining a fully inclusive educational environment for all learners regardless of ability or background.
Staff development. Has a clear commitment to the continuous professional development of all staff to ensure the highest educational standards.	**Communication.** An excellent communicator with the ability to effectively engage with teachers, pupils, parents and the wider community.
Vision. Has a clear strategic vision for continuous improvement to work with the governors and build on a school's strengths and successes.	**Performance management.** Expertise in the establishment of key performance indicators designed to monitor the overall performance of the school against clearly defined metrics.

SELECTED CAREER ACHIEVEMENTS

- Identified an opportunity to introduce a programme of continuing professional development for all teaching staff. Developed a relationship with a local university and provided day release for all staff. As a result, teaching standards improved and staff turnover was reduced.
- Secured additional funding from the local authority to provide an after-school facility for children suffering from dyslexia to receive specialist teaching. Provided further in-house training to teaching staff to ensure a cohesive approach to teaching children with special needs.

Now look on the next page at Rachel's CV at an earlier stage in her career. Notice that because she has less experience the career achievements are more limited, but they are still very focused on what will be especially relevant to her job search. At this earlier stage in her career the importance of her academic achievements, including her A levels, and the details of her degree are also emphasised. Nevertheless, the format is exactly the same as for her more senior-level CV shown above.

Rachel Arnold

32 Fontwell Drive, East Slendon, Wiltshire WA56 3TY
Telephone: 01234 567891
Email: rachel.arnold@email.com

Versatile teacher with 12 months' experience teaching year 5 children in a primary school. A fully qualified teacher with a BA (Hons) in Primary Education from Bangor University. An enthusiastic and committed teacher with a real passion for education and with additional experience of working with special needs children. Now seeking a role in a larger school with further opportunities for career development and with a focus on special needs and school management.

KEY SKILLS AND EXPERIENCE

BA (Hons) in Primary Education	Extracurricular activities including netball and football
Fully qualified teacher status	Member of the parent/teacher committee
12 months' work experience	Liaison with local authority for ESN funding
Additional experience in teaching special needs	Studying for MSc in Education and Training Management

SELECTED CAREER ACHIEVEMENTS

- BA in Primary Education with First Class Honours.
- Established the special needs unit at my primary school.
- Secured additional funding from the local authority for the ESN and dyslexia unit.
- Appointed as a teacher representative on the board of governors.
- Raised £250 by organising a parents and teachers fun run to buy books for the school library.

CAREER HISTORY

1999–2000
St Peters Primary School
Year 5 Classroom Teacher

- Teaching all areas of the curriculum.
- Classroom management/behaviour management.
- Planning and preparation of children's work.
- Assessment/marking/report-writing.

EDUCATION AND PROFESSIONAL QUALIFICATIONS

2000	Currently studying for MSc in Education and Training Management by distance learning
1999	BA (Hons) First Class, University of Bangor
1995	Graduated from Cardiff High School with A grades in English, History and Geography

ADDITIONAL INFORMATION

Nationality:	British
References:	Available on request

Example CV extract for a senior management role in sales and marketing

For jobs in sales and marketing, employers will be looking for evidence of your achievements. They'll want to know about how you have met your sales targets and how you measure the success of your sales and marketing campaigns.

James Madison

35 Ellsworth Drive, West Hayfield, Bucks TH16 9RA
Telephone: 01234 567891
Email: james.madison@email.com

A degree-qualified sales and marketing professional with over 10 years' broad experience in multi-channel customer-focused roles. A member of the Chartered Institute of Marketing with an outstanding track record of success working in an innovative and fast-paced commercial environment using online technology. Now seeking a challenging new role in the field of digital marketing in the UK or Europe.

KEY SKILLS AND EXPERIENCE

Sales and marketing manager. Experience of identifying and generating new business while developing and expanding existing business to successfully achieve agreed annual targets.

Digital marketing. Good experience gained through a variety of channels, including websites and social networking. Experience of search engine optimisation and the use of content management systems.

Leadership. Expertise in managing high-performing teams of sales and marketing professionals. Provides training and coaching to develop team skills.

Commercial focus. An entrepreneurial flair and a strong commercial awareness. Identifies opportunities for increased revenues.

International experience. Extensive work experience in Europe having led the digital marketing team at ASG Media based in Paris. Good experience of managing multinational teams and speaks fluent French and German.

Proposal development. Develops and presents customer proposals and responsible for presenting products and services to potential clients through direct communication in face-to-face meetings, telephone calls and emails.

Communication. Proven ability to communicate effectively with clients, senior managers, partners and personnel at all levels. Excellent written and spoken presentation skills in English, French and German.

Qualified. A BSc (Hons) in Marketing from the University of Leicester (2:i). A member of the Chartered Institute of Marketing.

SELECTED CAREER ACHIEVEMENTS

- Identified opportunities for new business with clients in the UK and Europe. Gathered requirements and wrote client proposals. Consistently achieved or exceeded personal revenue targets for over 3 years and twice received an award for the best monthly sales performance.
- Following my successful sales performance promoted to the position of Sales Manager with responsibility for a team of 10 people based in the UK and France. Turned around the performance of this team by providing training and coaching. Achieved the highest single team revenue figure for digital marketing sales at the end of 2012.

Example CV extract for a job in engineering

Ray Moore MBA

10 Ferry Road, North Warwick, Hants GU23 5RT,
United Kingdom
Telephone: 01234 567891
Email: ray.moore@email.com

Senior construction engineer with over 20 years' international experience of leading large-scale construction projects and consistently achieving performance goals. A qualified and energetic engineer with additional business development skills and a proven ability to add value to an employer's business development team. Now seeking a challenging new leadership role within the EMEA region.

KEY SKILLS AND EXPERIENCE

A qualified chartered engineer.	Client relationship management.
Experienced project manager.	Process management.
Leader of large international teams.	Expertise in project planning.
Bid management experience.	BSc in Construction, MBA.

SELECTED CAREER ACHIEVEMENTS

- Worked with the construction business team to identify opportunities. Wrote bids for contracts in a number of emerging markets in Africa and the Middle East. Assembled and managed bid teams and won a number of major contracts for construction projects ranging in value from $10 million to over $100 million. Played a key role in negotiating terms with clients following the successful award of contracts.
- Assigned to turn around an underperforming construction development. Undertook a comprehensive review and then put in place a robust remedial action plan and took personal charge of the assignment. Regained the confidence of the client and subsequently delivered the project on schedule and within the agreed budget. Received a personal letter of commendation from the CEO.

Example CV extract for a chief executive

Alison Hyde MBA

22 London Road, Harwick, Dorset DH13 7YH
Telephone: 01234 567891
Email: alison.hyde@email.com

Experienced chief executive with over 30 years' experience in the transport and logistics sectors and with a demonstrable track record of success in high-profile leadership roles. A qualified chartered accountant with an INSEAD MBA and with significant experience of leading large, complex organisations and delivering sustainable business growth. An inspirational leader with strategic insight and the proven ability to foster a high-performing working environment. Seeking a challenging new role that will enable me to influence and effect positive change.

KEY SKILLS AND EXPERIENCE

Chief executive. A consistent track record of achievement as chief executive within large, complex service delivery organisations in the field of international transport and logistics.	**Financial management.** Takes full responsibility for ensuring robust financial management and control of operations. Provides leadership in planning, accounting and budgeting.
Strategic management. Outstanding ability to provide insight and vision and, with the board of directors, sets and implements strategy and enables the organisation to achieve its full potential.	**Change management.** Very extensive experience of managing change and business transformation. Restructuring organisations and establishing processes and structures to effectively meet market needs.
Leadership. Expertise in leading and inspiring up to 500 multi-disciplined staff. Provides clear and visible leadership and fosters a high-performance culture.	**Communication.** Outstanding ability to communicate effectively with customers and shareholders. The credibility to engage with both the board and staff at every level.
Commercial focus. An entrepreneurial flair and a strong commercial awareness. Identifies new business opportunities, engages with clients and enables the organisation to achieve its commercial goals.	**Qualified.** A First Class Honours degree in Economics from the University of Cambridge. An INSEAD MBA and a qualified chartered accountant. Currently studying for a PhD in International Transportation at Cambridge.

SELECTED CAREER ACHIEVEMENTS

- Faced with the challenge of expanding international operations at Simpson Logistics, I was responsible for leading the company's bid to win a major deal for a transport contract with a US-based telecommunications business. Assembled a multi-disciplined bid team of 50 people and developed the bid. Negotiated the award of the contract with a value of US $50 million over 5 years.
- Following the acquisition of another UK-based company operating in the air transport sector, restructured Simpson Logistics to absorb 350 new staff and additionally consolidated three regional offices into a single new headquarters building in central London. As a direct result of the acquisition, increased market share by 25% and further increased revenues from US $150 to US $200 million in only 3 years.

Writing a CV after a break in your career

There could be any number of reasons why there might be a gap in your CV. Perhaps you have been away from work for a long period of time while bringing up your children. You may have been taking a sabbatical or a planned career break. Or you may simply have been out of work. In each of these examples you should simply state the circumstances surrounding your time away from work and write it up on your CV as you would for a regular job. Under no circumstances should you attempt to cover up time away from work by 'inventing' jobs or extending dates. This is not only illegal but you will be found out. Most employers nowadays do take up references, check dates and question you closely about your career history. Honesty is the best policy!

What you can do quite legitimately is to put the dates that you finished working for an employer contractually. It's sometimes the case that people are made redundant (or laid off) immediately and told to take 'gardening leave'. Although technically you are at home and looking for a new job you are still employed until your contract of employment comes to an end. Many managers are on 3 months' or even 6 months' notice these days – if you finished working in July 2012 but your contract terminated at the end of October, it is quite acceptable for you to put the end date for that job as October 2012.

If you have been unemployed for 3 months then it's perfectly acceptable to say that you have been looking for work during this period. The average time to find a job is 3–6 months so there is nothing unusual about this. Remember there is no longer any stigma attached to being made redundant or being unemployed; unfortunately it is commonplace these days. The recruiter or employer reviewing your CV may well have been unemployed themself at some point in their career or at least know someone who has.

EMPLOYMENT HISTORY

September 2005 – Present

- Took a planned career break to provide full-time care for my two children.
- Played an active role in managing my children's school as a governor.
- Served as a committee member with a local charity.
- Raised over £2,000 by taking part in a charity skydive in aid of Cancer Research.

July 2000 – August 2005

Marketing Manager

Richmond Technology Ltd

UK-based company providing innovative digital marketing and communications solutions for the financial services sector

- Developed and implemented the corporate communications strategy and supporting programmes.
- Delivered a number of high-impact communications and engagement campaigns.
- Influenced the senior management team to adopt best communication practice.
- Selected and oversaw the development of effective marketing and communications using appropriate channels to achieve measurable business results.
- Developed the new corporate website and, from fewer than 5,000 monthly visitors in 2004, increased the number of visits to an average of 20,000 per month in 2005. (Source: *Google Analytics*)

Note that the career break is treated as a normal part of your employment history. Adding some additional information about what you have been doing will reassure the employer that although you have been at home you have also been maintaining your professional skills by getting involved with the running of your children's school or serving on the committee of a local charity.

EMPLOYMENT HISTORY

December 2011 – Present

- Planned career break.
- Undertook a personal project to renovate a house.
- Worked with an architect to draw up plans and obtain planning permission.
- Acted as project manager coordinating the activities of multiple tradesmen.
- Completed the renovation project on schedule and within budget.

As can be seen in the example given above, even time off to undertake a personal project to renovate a house can be presented professionally on your CV. In this example there is also an indication that the candidate acted as a project manager and completed the project on schedule and within budget – clearly very relevant professional skills.

If you have been made redundant (or laid off) you can also include this information in your CV as part of your career history. Simply state that you were made redundant and include information about what you have been doing during your period of unemployment.

EMPLOYMENT HISTORY

September 2012 – Present
- Career break following redundancy from Carter Technology.
- Undertook voluntary work with a local charity.
- Updated professional skills and achieved additional technical certification in software testing.

The online CV

Apart from having a regular CV document which you can upload to job sites and send to recruiters by email, there is another option: having an online CV on your personal website. This can look extremely professional and has the advantage that your personal details can be found easily by anyone using a search engine such as Google.

Now, if you are just conducting a regular job search and expect to be employed within a few weeks and then have no further need for a CV, this option is probably not for you. However, if you are a consultant or contractor who is regularly looking for work or if you are working in a profession where you need to showcase your professional background, then an online CV could be the right option.

Using WordPress or a similar free resource, it is possible to obtain a suitable CV (or résumé) theme or website template and create a very professional-looking online CV which could either stand alone or form part of your personal website. You would also have the option to buy (if available) a domain name containing your name, for example www.John-Smith.com.

Of course, you can also use a platform such as LinkedIn (www.linkedin.com) to place your professional profile and experience online. We'll discuss using LinkedIn as a job search resource in Chapter 4.

Have a look at an example of an online CV at www.my-online-profile.com.

Creating a video CV

Another way to support your online presence would be to create a video CV. The very easy way to do this would be to set up your own video camera or even the video camera in your phone and start recording. Open an account with YouTube and you can upload your video. You can then paste the URL for your YouTube video straight into your regular CV document and then recruiters can click on the link and actually see you talking about your career or perhaps a specific recent project. This is certainly an interesting option and the facility to see a candidate for a job 'in action' might well be enough to get you an interview.

But beware – a poor-quality video might have the opposite effect. A badly made video might suggest that you also have a slapdash attitude to your work, and while some people seem to be natural performers on video, other people, who would impress face to face, somehow don't come across on camera.

If you are determined to try this option then be sure to get an opinion from a trusted friend or colleague before including a video with your CV. Having a video CV is not going to be appropriate for every job category and, in particular, for a regular job search it may not warrant the investment in time and effort. However, there are some scenarios where having a video CV would be beneficial to you. If you are a contractor, interim manager or freelance consultant then being able to showcase your abilities on a video might just give you a margin over others. These types of jobs often have to be filled at short notice and hiring decisions are sometimes made on the basis of a telephone interview or very brief face-to-face meeting. That video, perhaps describing a recent assignment, might just make a difference.

If you are looking for work overseas, the logistics of interviewing candidates is often quite challenging. Employers have to consider having an extended telephone interview or perhaps flying candidates to the work location. Being able to provide a video CV might get you a job offer ahead of other candidates relying on a traditional CV.

3 SEARCHING FOR JOBS

Now it's time to start putting your CV to work. With a well written CV you are now ready to actually start searching for jobs. Of course you can search the newspapers and the internet but there are quite a number of other sources of jobs, many of which are not advertised and will therefore attract fewer applications. With the emergence of social media there are new opportunities to extend your job search and perhaps get a head start on the majority of job hunters who are searching only through the traditional channels.

This chapter will help you:

■ identify the main channels for your job search

■ decide which newspapers will advertise jobs that suit your professional background

■ decide which internet job sites are best for your job search

■ use professional networking sites in your job search

■ use social media (including Twitter and Facebook) in your job search.

The different job search channels

We have seen that there are a number of channels for your job search. These include:

- jobs advertised in the press
- jobs advertised on the internet
- jobs found through recruitment agencies
- jobs found via your networking activities
- jobs found via social media
- jobs found at recruitment events or career fairs.

Searching for jobs advertised in the press

You can search for jobs in the press, including all of the national newspapers plus any specialist or trade journals that relate specifically to your industry or profession. For the most senior roles in the UK the first place to look would be *The Sunday Times* Appointments section. Blue-chip employers looking to recruit senior executives in both the public and private sectors very often use *The Sunday Times*. The other broadsheet newspapers also advertise a wide range of jobs in different categories and you should be aware of the specific types of vacancies advertised on each day of the week. In the UK the *Guardian, Telegraph, Independent* and *The Times* advertise certain types of vacancy on particular days of the week (see page 228).

With the exception of *The Sunday Times* (which focuses on senior appointments), you can also find jobs at every level and in a much wider range of job categories by searching the jobs sections of the newspapers' websites. Here's a list of those sites that include vacancies at every level from graduate to CEO:

- *Guardian/Observer* – http://jobs.guardian.co.uk
- *Independent* – http://ijobs.independent.co.uk/jobs; http://independent.graduate-jobs.com
- *The Times* – http://jobs.thetimes.co.uk
- *Telegraph* – http://jobs.telegraph.co.uk

The possible disadvantage of job advertisements in the press is the sheer volume of responses that can be expected. The more positive aspect is that job advertisements in the press are generally more costly and take some time to format and prepare. For that reason it is highly likely that the job that you are applying for will be real. Because responding to an advertisement in the press is going to be significantly more competitive, you should have an even higher motivation to make sure that your application is perfect and will stand out from all the other applications.

When reviewing a press advertisement make sure that you check very carefully that you do actually have all the skills, experience and qualifications required. Because of the volume of responses, recruiters will be particularly strict in only shortlisting candidates who have all or most of the required experience. Remember the advice given in Chapter 2 on creating your CV. Try to put key information that matches you to a particular role at the top of page one of the CV so that it is easy for the recruiter to match your skills and experience to the role.

Very often jobs advertised in the press will also require some kind of covering letter to accompany the CV. On occasion you may still be required to apply for a job advertised in the press by regular post. In that case your covering letter will take the form of a hard-copy letter; however, more often these days you will be invited to write the covering letter as an email or alternatively you will be able to add a covering letter to an online application. You can use the covering letter to immediately highlight to the recruiter the specific skills, qualifications and experience that you have that match the requirements specified in the job advertisement.

In the covering letter introduce yourself, then state your interest in the position in no more than three short paragraphs; outline the skills, experience and qualifications that make you ideal for the position, and then refer the reader to your CV for further details. Consider underlining specific words and phrases in your CV or putting them in bold. For example, if the job advertisement requires you to be a qualified chartered accountant then you can embolden this information in your CV. If the job advertisement specifies that you must speak fluent French, then again embolden this information in your CV. Remember that you want to make the recruiter's job as easy as possible!

Searching for jobs advertised on the internet

Most people are aware that the internet is a hugely important resource for job hunters. Apart from the opportunity to search for jobs you can use the internet in a number of different ways in order to raise your professional profile and make your details easier to find for both employers and recruiters.

Using the internet you can:

- search for jobs on internet job sites
- register your personal details on internet job sites to receive details of suitable jobs
- upload your CV so that it is visible to recruiters
- search for jobs, and possibly upload your CV, on company (employer) websites
- search for jobs using social media such as Facebook and Twitter
- use professional networking sites such as LinkedIn.

The first thing you should consider is uploading your CV to some of the internet job sites. Most of the sites have this facility and it's well worth doing. The main job sites are a prime source of candidates for most recruiters and employers, so you definitely don't want to miss the opportunity of being found on the internet by this route. An important tip here is to make sure that you regularly refresh your CV on the job site. Most recruiters tend to search for CVs that have been added to the site recently on the assumption that these will be the most active job seekers. So make sure that you either refresh your CV or take it down and upload it again on a regular basis; this way your CV will always come up in the recruiters' searches for recently added CVs.

Here are some of the major internet job sites in the UK that you might use both to search for jobs and to register or upload your CV.

Reed (www.reed.co.uk)
Reed claims to be the UK's number one internet job site with over 125,000 live jobs advertised in most parts of the UK in different categories and sectors.

Reed also advertises international jobs and provides useful information on training courses (and qualifications) in a wide range of professional fields.

Jobsite (www.jobsite.co.uk)

Jobsite is one of the leading internet job sites and has a huge range of jobs in almost every job category and at every level from school leaver/graduate all the way up to the most senior management jobs.

Total Jobs (www.totaljobs.com)

Total Jobs is another very large internet job site that has a very wide range of jobs at every level. It has powerful search capabilities and options to search for jobs within a certain distance of your postcode. You can also find international jobs on the Total Jobs site.

Monster (www.monster.co.uk)

Monster is by far the biggest job site in the world and there are many international jobs advertised. You can search for jobs in a specific location so, for example, you can refine your search to include jobs in finance in London with salaries in excess of £50,000. Monster is a major resource for recruiters as there are more than 13 million CVs stored on the site.

A quick review of the internet will show you that there are many different internet job sites that may be more or less suitable for your needs. For example, there are sites that focus on specific types of jobs covering almost every job category and sector. Some examples are given below.

Exec Appointments (www.exec-appointments.com)

This site is owned by the UK's *Financial Times*. Here you will find any number of more senior executive roles in a range of different sectors at salaries ranging from £50,000 a year to above £250,000 a year. There are also international roles.

eFinancial Careers (www.efinancialcareers.co.uk)

If you are looking specifically for roles in the finance world then this is the site for you. There are finance roles in just about every discipline, including senior roles in investment banking, and again there is a significant number of international roles.

CW Jobs (www.cwjobs.co.uk)

This site lists IT jobs covering everything from roles in IT project management to roles for software engineers and technical architects.

There's a longer listing of internet job sites (including specialist sites) in Chapter 10.

You don't have to register or upload your CV in order to search for jobs; however, it will make the process of actually applying for a job from the job site much simpler if you do register first and upload your CV to the site. Remember that just because you have uploaded your CV to a job site does not mean that everyone can see it. You have complete control and, like Facebook, you can choose to make your personal data public or not.

Another interesting source of jobs on the internet would be the various job sites that aggregate jobs from a wide number of different job sites. These sites crawl over all of the job sites (over 600 job sites in the UK) and bring them to you all in one place, usually listing over a million vacancies. These sites may also list jobs advertised on employer websites. A good example of an aggregate site is www.indeed.co.uk.

You can search the aggregate job sites in exactly the same way as you would use the main job sites. The advantage is that they will search many lesser known job sites that may be used by smaller organisations or regional sites that advertise jobs locally to your area. A list of aggregate job sites can be found in Chapter 10.

Registering with the job sites

Most of the internet job sites provide the facility to register your contact details; you can then receive regular emails that relate to jobs that you specify. This is a very useful facility which means that you do not have to keep searching the sites on a daily basis. If you set up your search correctly then you will receive notification of all relevant jobs that match your search criteria. Remember that simply registering your details does not mean that you have to upload your CV or make your CV public.

Uploading your CV to job sites

Beyond simply registering with the major job sites you can also upload your CV. You can then use the site in one of two ways. You can simply upload your CV (or in some cases several different versions of your CV) and then make applications for jobs that have been advertised on that site. You will have a paper trail in the form of a confirmation email from the site each time you apply for a job. But you also have the option to make your CV public and then enable recruiters and employers to approach you directly and consider you for jobs, some of which may not have been advertised. Most recruiters search the main job sites on a daily basis. You should be aware that if you do not want people to see your details you can control this feature and deactivate your CV at any time.

It's important to be fully conversant with the process for uploading your CV to an internet job site and deciding whether it should be visible or not. Although all of the job sites have slightly different processes for registering and uploading your CV, they all have the option to make your CV visible or not.

If you do *not* want your CV to be visible then remember to deselect the box marked 'Allow recruiters to search for your CV' (or similar wording depending on the job site). This box is generally ticked by default so it's important to uncheck this box if you are planning to use the site only for your own job searches and applications and do not want recruiters to be able to search for your CV. You can go back to this option at any time if you change your mind.

There are a number of issues to consider when uploading your CV and making it visible on an internet job site. You are going to make your personal details and the fact that you are looking for a new job very public. It may seem an obvious point but don't upload your CV (and make it visible) until you are ready to start your job search. If you are still working then you will probably not want to publicise the fact that you are looking for an alternative position. If you are simply working out your notice or you have already informed your employer that you intend to leave then this is not going to be a problem.

Remember that at any time you can delete or temporarily suspend your CV on the job sites. If you are going away or you are at the final interview stage for a job then you probably won't want to receive frequent calls from recruiters. Of course, if you want to start receiving calls once more then you can easily make your CV visible again.

As mentioned earlier, you should consider creating a special email address and using a separate mobile number so that you can keep your job search communications separate from your personal communications.

In addition to the internet job sites, you should also remember that many of the recruitment agencies will have lists of vacancies on their own websites and the facility to register your CV and apply for jobs directly with them. A list of some of the leading recruitment agencies and headhunters can be found in Chapter 10. Additionally, you can of course search the websites of employers directly. Many larger organisations also have the facility to search for jobs in different categories and to register and upload your CV.

TOTAL JOB SEARCH TIP

Get a separate email address and mobile phone number for your job search.

The importance of keywords

Refer back to the section in the last chapter on using keywords in your CV (see page 58) because this is what will enable recruiters to find your CV in a search. Again, think carefully about the likely keywords that will be used in a search for candidates with your background and experience. Keep checking advertisements and check the kind of language, words and phrases that are commonly used in job advertisements for jobs that interest you and make sure that those words and phrases are used in your CV. Many of the job sites allow you to provide a brief summary of your experience which will become the 'thumbnail' description that the recruiter will see before they actually open your CV document. That summary needs to be written using keywords that will be found in a search and will grab the attention of the recruiter. An abbreviated version of your CV profile will probably be about the right length for this brief summary of your experience.

What response will I get if I allow recruiters to search for my CV?

Be prepared to receive quite a number of calls that will *not* be relevant to your job search. Be polite but make sure that you pre-qualify each job that a recruiter calls to discuss. The recruiter may have pulled up 50 or more candidate CVs in a search and will be working through a long list of possible candidates for a job quite quickly. The recruiter will be under time pressure and therefore will welcome a relatively quick exchange of information to establish whether or not the role is going to be suitable.

This conversation can start with some fairly standard queries. For example, you could ask the following.

- What's the location of the job?
- What's the job title?
- What's the salary/package?

If the answers to these basic queries are acceptable then you can move on to more detailed queries.

- What are the key responsibilities?
- What's the reporting line?
- What are the essential skills and experience required?
- What qualifications (if any) are required?

And so on . . .

This type of exchange can take just a few minutes but will save you from wasting your time having a lengthy conversation about a job that subsequently turns out to be unsuitable.

There are some actions that you can take to reduce the number of calls about unsuitable jobs. First of all you can include your full address (including your zip code or postcode) on your CV and make it clear that you will only be willing to work within reasonable commuting distance of that location. Many recruiters undertake 'proximity searches' on the job sites. This means that they specify in their search that they wish to view only the CVs of candidates who live within a set distance from the work location. Putting your full address (or at least your postcode) on your CV should ensure that you don't get called for jobs that are too far away.

You should also note that you can upload your CV to the internet sites of some national newspapers. This facility is available with the following newspapers in the UK:

- *Guardian* – http://jobs.guardian.co.uk/profile
- *Telegraph* – http://jobs.telegraph.co.uk
- *The Times* – http://appointments.thesundaytimes.co.uk/cvmatch.

Searching for jobs using LinkedIn

The internet job sites are by no means the only internet resources available to you. In addition to the job sites you should also consider using LinkedIn (www. linkedin.com), which is the professional equivalent of Facebook for business. LinkedIn is a *free* resource and you have the same facility as with the job sites to register and upload your CV. LinkedIn is used extensively by recruiters to search for candidates for jobs on a global basis.

Within LinkedIn you also have the facility to join professional groups. For example, there are professional groups for project managers (the Project Manager Network) or telecom professionals (Telecom Professionals). Joining these groups will enable you to make contact with other professionals in your field (in your own country and globally) and to exchange information and also to learn about possible job opportunities.

You can also use LinkedIn to ensure that recruiters can find your details online. Using the groups you can actively network with other members to find out about new job opportunities or to hear about organisations that may be recruiting professionals in your field. Many blue-chip organisations use LinkedIn either to search for new staff or to advertise vacancies.

It's now considered almost essential for business professionals to have a LinkedIn profile. Every Fortune 500 company and every FTSE 100 company has LinkedIn members and it's also worth noting that there are over 130,000 recruiters (worldwide) who are also members of LinkedIn. You can also easily search LinkedIn to find former colleagues or potential new contacts who may be able to help you find a new job.

Register with www.linkedin.com and create your profile. We'll discuss optimising your LinkedIn profile for job searching in a lot more detail in Chapter 4.

Once you have registered you can start to search for jobs on LinkedIn in exactly the same way that you would search on the internet job sites. Just click on the 'Find Jobs' tab at the top of the LinkedIn home page. You can enter keywords and a job title to begin your search and also choose to view jobs within a set distance of your location. Once you identify a suitable job you can apply and attach your CV and covering letter.

LinkedIn has become a major resource for recruiters all over the world. If you have a strong profile and CV on LinkedIn you can expect to start receiving calls from recruiters. Be sure to monitor the keywords in your profile. Recruiters will almost certainly be using the search facility in LinkedIn to identify suitable candidates for their clients.

TOTAL JOB SEARCH TIP

Sign up to LinkedIn and search for jobs.

Searching for jobs through recruitment agencies

If you apply for a job these days the chances are that you may be applying through a recruitment agency. What should you expect from an agency or individual consultant?

Let's assume that you have applied for a job advertised by a recruitment agency on one of the job sites. You should receive either an immediate automated response or a personal response within a few hours acknowledging that your application has been received. You should be concerned if you don't receive any kind of acknowledgement. How long should you wait before following up? I would suggest two working days; however, if you genuinely feel that you are uniquely well qualified for the job, then call sooner. If you are quite sure that you are a perfect match for the job then a good consultant will probably already have called you. Ideally you will have sent a CV that was specifically tailored to the role so that it will be a very easy decision for the consultant to pick out your CV and give you a call.

If you have the right experience then a professional consultant will want to interview you for the job. Treat this agency interview in exactly the same way as you would a 'proper' interview with an employer. The consultant may well have a long list of up to 10 candidates and will want to see who will be the best fit for the employer. Good recruitment consultants know their clients extremely well and in some cases are trusted to the point that they will be allowed to conduct the first interview on behalf of the client. Do try to attend a face-to-face interview as this will always give you the advantage over candidates who can only commit to a telephone interview. Making the effort to attend the agency interview will also demonstrate your motivation and commitment.

TOTAL JOB SEARCH TIP

Try to attend face-to-face interviews with selected recruitment agencies.

Attending face-to-face interviews will also ensure that you carefully consider which jobs to apply for. I would strongly recommend that you apply only for jobs where you are certain you have all or most of the skills required. If the advertisement says 'in-depth experience of credit analysis in the retail banking sector', don't apply if you have been working in a sales role in telecommunications!

This agency interview can serve a dual purpose as once you have convinced the consultant that you are right for the role, they will want to give you a thorough briefing on what to expect at the subsequent employer interview. Remember that the consultant may have had several candidates who have already attended interviews for similar roles with the same employer. The consultant can brief you in detail on the organisation, the working environment, the other people in the department and most especially the interviewer or interviewers. What sort of interview questions can you expect? Will this be a formal or informal interview? Will you need to make a presentation?

Once the recruitment consultant confirms that you have been shortlisted for interview, make sure that you get their assurance that your CV will be submitted to the client. Make a note of exactly when your CV was sent together with the name of the client. Don't give your permission for your CV to be sent anywhere unless you know where it is being sent. This can lead to potentially embarrassing instances of your CV being submitted to the same client by two different agencies. Keep a record and don't let this happen. As previously suggested, you should maintain a simple spreadsheet of all the jobs that you have applied for, when you applied, the name of the recruitment agency and contact, and perhaps a note of the version of the CV that you sent. Ask the consultant when you can expect a decision regarding an interview, put a reminder of the date in your schedule and be sure to follow it up.

Hopefully all of this should lead to a face-to-face interview or interviews with the employer. Let's assume that you have been successful and the client has decided to make you a job offer. Your consultant should be able to guide you through the whole offer process. Make sure that you are completely open about your current earnings and be absolutely clear about what salary and package you are expecting. There is nothing worse than getting an offer and then finding that it is for much less than you had expected. Be upfront about this early on and make sure that the consultant understands exactly what you are looking for and there should be no confusion.

Selecting the right recruitment consultants

You should try to build trusting relationships with several different recruitment consultants. Bear in mind that the vast majority of employers will pass their recruitment requirements to external agencies so you will invariably have to work through a recruitment agency, at least initially, when you apply for a job. A good recruitment consultant can make your job search much easier and will provide you with advice and will potentially be a key ally in your search for a new job.

How do you identify a 'good' recruitment consultant? First of all start looking at which recruiters are consistently advertising jobs in your field. Many recruitment agencies will have teams who specialise in very specific types of roles, for example investment banking, IT, legal, HR or financial services. You will also find specialist agencies who deal only with IT roles or HR roles, and within those agencies you will find individual consultants who recruit only IT project managers or corporate lawyers or qualified accountants. Your initial task is to identify those individuals and then contact them and stay in touch with them. If you have the right skills then these consultants can help you and will want to meet you.

How do you know if they truly understand your field? Ask them which companies they deal with. You will soon get a feel for their level of expertise. Many recruiters (particularly at the more senior level) will have actually worked in a particular sector so they should have real inside knowledge. If you want to check up on a recruitment consultant's background, then the chances are that they will have a profile on a professional networking site such as LinkedIn.

Headhunters

It's usually the case that a headhunter will approach you; unlike the conventional recruitment agency they will not generally accept unsolicited CVs. That said, some of the larger headhunter firms do occasionally advertise jobs on their websites (rather than in the press or generally on the internet) and it's always worth looking to see if there might be a suitable opportunity.

However, most headhunters operate differently. They take a very detailed brief from a client and undertake research to find suitable candidates. The research is much less likely to be on the job sites and much more likely to be about researching individuals who may be working at the most senior levels within organisations and, importantly, are not currently looking for a new job.

How can I get headhunted?

As already suggested, you need to be visible in order to attract the attention of a recruiter or headhunter. Networking, using social media (Twitter and Facebook) and using LinkedIn are very good ways for you to increase your presence and therefore become a potential target for a headhunter.

Becoming 'famous' in your field is important. You can offer to speak at industry conferences, or write interesting and informative articles in the national or trade press or in a blog. You need to build your profile to the point where you are perceived to be an authority in your particular field. It doesn't matter what that field is, whether it's banking and finance, information technology, law or sales and marketing, if you have something interesting to say then broadcast to as wide an audience as you can.

Headhunters tend to specialise in specific sectors or disciplines, so if you are a private banker then search out the headhunters who operate in that specific field. Once you have identified the few individuals who operate exclusively in your field, make contact and start building a relationship.

If you are currently employed and not looking to change your job immediately then there is a useful tactic to consider. Assuming you are in a position to recruit staff, think about giving the headhunter an assignment; ask them to recruit for you. This will certainly help you to build a professional relationship with the headhunter and when at some point in the future you start looking for another position you will already have a useful contact. Another possibility would be to try to find out what sort of candidates the headhunter is looking for currently. If you are well connected in your field then offer to provide the names of individuals who you know are capable and could be suitable. Headhunters talk on a daily basis to their contacts and listen in to the latest news. Who is the star performer at that particular bank? Who is rumoured to be looking for another job? Become one of those contacts and the likelihood is that the next time the headhunter has a job that might be suitable, you will be the first person that they will call.

Searching for jobs using social media

If you are not already registered with Twitter then I suggest that you register now. For the purposes of your job search it's best to keep your Twitter username professional, so try to avoid any eccentric or unusual names. Complete the sign-up process and click 'Create my account'. At this point you can add a photo and some details to your Twitter profile. You have 160 characters and you should try to use the right keywords to make sure that your details are found by potential employers and recruiters who are searching Twitter for candidates for jobs. The profile in your CV will be a little too long but you can modify your existing profile to produce an effective Twitter profile.

For example:

A UK qualified chartered accountant with an INSEAD MBA and with excellent experience in strategic management and a proven ability to evaluate and control operational costs and margins.

Be prepared to modify your Twitter profile and constantly review job advertisements so that you use the right keywords that will be found by recruiters searching Twitter.

You can also start searching some of your other online accounts to find out if you already have contacts who are using Twitter. You can search on Gmail, Yahoo, Hotmail, AOL and LinkedIn. You can also simply search Twitter for other users by name. You can start following other users and tweeting yourself; as you start following other people some will also follow you, and as you tweet people will begin to follow your tweets. Remember that you are limited to only 140 characters per tweet.

Make sure that your tweets are positive and relevant to your job search. You can begin by letting your followers know that you are available and looking for work. You may well receive information about jobs. Perhaps one of your Twitter followers has previously worked for a company that you would like to approach; could they provide you with a contact name? Search Twitter for contacts who may be able to help you in your job search. Start following recruiters, headhunters, HR directors or other professionals directly involved in recruitment in your field, and follow individuals who share a professional interest. If you are an IT project manager with expertise in Oracle HR then search for that term and see who's out there with the same or similar experience. Similarly, if you are a mergers and acquisitions professional with specialist knowledge of the retail sector then start following people in that field. Remember that the great advantage of Twitter is that you can connect with anyone you choose anywhere in the world. Look at people's bios and, if they work in a field that is of interest to you, follow them or get in touch.

Many recruitment consultants (and some of the internet job sites) tweet their latest vacancies using Twitter. Find recruiters and job sites that specialise in your field and start following them to be sure of seeing their latest vacancies. From some of the job sites you'll get a stream of jobs, many of which will not be suitable, but if you search for and follow @jobsitejobs on Twitter you can receive personalised job tweets. After you have followed @jobsitejobs, check your Twitter inbox for a direct message from Jobsite and click on the link. You can then select keywords, location and salary expectations so that you only receive tweets relevant to your job search.

There are also a number of useful websites that you can search for jobs via Twitter, including:

- www.tweetmyjobs.com
- www.twitjobsearch.com.

If you have a personal website or blog then put the link into your tweets. If you don't yet have a personal website or blog then at least set up a LinkedIn profile (www.linkedin.com) which you can then add to your tweets. Because your LinkedIn address is quite long, use http://tinyurl.com to create a shorter link so that you don't use up all your 140 characters in your tweet. Use the right keywords in your tweets. If you are an IT helpdesk analyst with experience in supporting networks, tweet about networking and always include a link to your personal website, blog or LinkedIn profile.

You can use a number of different hashtags (#) for your job search. The most popular is #jobs, but this is rather generalist and will very soon start to clog up your Twitter feed with mostly unsuitable jobs from around the world. There are more specific hashtags that will help you to narrow your search: try #ukjobs, #itjobs, #accountancyjobs, #mediajobs, #salesjobs and many other similar categories.

Think about identifying a number of different recruiters who seem to consistently advertise jobs that are in your area of expertise. Follow them and continue to tweet on topics that reinforce your professional expertise. The chances are that they will contact you. Remember also that you can link your Twitter account to your LinkedIn profile.

Using Facebook in your job search

Although most people use Facebook for connecting and keeping up to date with friends, it can also be a useful networking tool for your job search. Place a note on Facebook explaining that you are available and looking for work. Your Facebook contacts may be your friends but do you know where they all work? Could that Facebook friend from the football club actually turn out to be the recruitment manager for a company where you would like to work? Of course Facebook is a platform to enhance people's social life, but it's still reasonable for you to ask for advice or contacts from your friends just as you might mention that you are looking for work when speaking to a friend face to face.

You can also use Facebook as a tool for your research prior to an interview; for example, place a note saying I'm going for an interview at ABC Company tomorrow, does anyone know someone who works there? Remember that as well as individuals, lots of companies now have Facebook pages where you can find further information about the company, its culture, key personalities and other background information that may not be available on their public website.

Don't forget to check your privacy settings on Facebook and be careful of what you post in your public profile. Remember that many recruiters and employers use Facebook to carry out checks on potential employees. There are plenty of examples of jobs that have been lost or job offers revoked because of inappropriate Facebook content. Be careful!

Other ways to search for jobs using Facebook

You can look at the Facebook Marketplace, which contains some job advertisements. Although it is not very well known and not very extensive, this may work to your advantage as fewer people will be applying for the jobs. It's certainly worth looking at on a regular basis.

Another possibility would be to place your own advertisement on Facebook. This works in the same way as Google AdWords and you will pay on the basis of the number of clicks on your advertisement. Facebook often offers £25 of free advertising so this may be an option worth trying at either no cost or minimal cost.

4 NETWORKING

We all know the old adage 'it's not what you know but who you know'. Networking as it relates to your job search is all about increasing the number of people *who you know* and therefore increasing your chances of finding a new job. Remember that networking is not just for senior business executives. Networking can be used at any stage in your career; through effective networking students and graduates can find opportunities for work experience or an internship that might well lead to permanent job offers. Networking also provides access to opportunities that may not be advertised and almost certainly will give you access to jobs where there is significantly less competition than the advertised jobs route.

This chapter will help you:

- understand the importance of networking as part of your job search

- identify potential network contacts

- grow your network of contacts

- develop your unique elevator pitch to your network contacts

- optimise your personal brand

- use online resources to enable others to network and contact you.

Build your network

As a first step you should list your close contacts. Your close contacts may be family members, close friends and colleagues. The next level should be a list of your acquaintances. In this list could be your business contacts and people you have met at business conferences, business meetings and so on.

From these initial lists you can start to prioritise your contacts and identify your objective in speaking to each contact. Start with your close contacts who you know will be friendly and helpful.

The next stage in your networking activities should be to start *building* your network of contacts. You can do this in a number of ways. Many of us already have some sort of online contacts list created via Facebook. Now would be a very good time to start extending these contacts using a professional networking tool such as LinkedIn (see Chapter 3 for more information on how to use LinkedIn for your job search). There are several other networking resources available including your local Chamber of Commerce. Chambers of Commerce frequently run networking events and this would be a good venue to meet people who may be able to help you with your job search. The Federation of Small Businesses (FSB) also holds regular meetings and networking events. There are other organisations that you might consider joining including the Bright Network (www.brightnetwork.co.uk), a careers network for students, graduates and young professionals.

These organisations (and there are many more) will provide you with the opportunity to make new contacts and build your network of contacts.

Your networking activities can be both active and passive. Your active networking will involve going out and meeting people, exchanging contact information and so on. But networking can also be passive whereby you create a presence and people come to you. We'll examine passive networking in more detail later in this chapter (see page 109).

Approaching your contacts

With reference to your active networking you should also consider *how* you are going to approach your contacts. This initial approach might be via a phone call, an email or letter, or perhaps via an invitation to connect on a networking site such as LinkedIn. Start constructing different letters, emails or brief LinkedIn invitations *now*.

Clearly you are going to approach people you already know (your close contacts) differently to your acquaintances (e.g. people you have met but don't know particularly well). Probably the best advice here is to be brief and make your point as clearly and succinctly as possible. Before you write, sit back and think carefully about what you want to achieve. It may be that you are writing specifically to ask if there might be job opportunities within the contact's organisation. You can write a brief paragraph introducing yourself (perhaps reminding the recipient of where you have met previously) and add a clear statement about your situation and that you may be available for the right opportunity. So that your letter/email does not seem like a job application I would advise you not to include your CV with this first contact but rather to offer to send the CV later if requested.

The outcome of this first contact may be one of the following:

- no response (in which case follow up after a week or so)
- an outright rejection (i.e. can't help)
- an offer to pass your details on to someone else (a referral)
- an offer to meet or at least to speak
- a positive invitation to attend an interview for a job.

With the exception of the first and second items, each of these responses represents a positive result in your networking activities. Instead of approaching your contacts in writing you may prefer to make contact by phone. This kind of approach would obviously be particularly appropriate for your close contacts (i.e. family and friends) but may also be appropriate for your acquaintances.

As you develop your networking activities you will also start to build a list of **referral contacts**, that is to say contacts that you have been referred to by other people. For example, you call a close contact or acquaintance who says that they cannot help but will pass your details on to someone else who may be able to help.

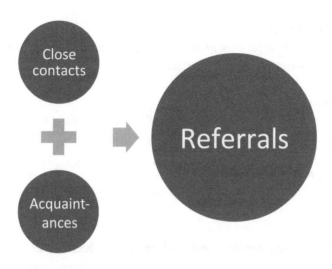

However, since these referral contacts won't have met you or spoken to you previously it would be as well to do some research before the call. Think in terms of the profile on your CV and you will have the right words. Start to think now about developing your two-minute **elevator pitch**. If the contact says 'Tell me about yourself' you need to have an effective pitch which is well prepared. It's well worth scripting your pitch (or at least making careful notes) so that you make the most of what may be a brief conversation with a key contact who can help you with your job search. Much better to be prepared than to put the phone down and realise that you forgot to mention some important information.

Guidelines for a pitch to a new network contact

Introduce yourself
'Hello, my name is John Smith.'

Your professional role
'I'm a very experienced sales and marketing manager.'

Your education and qualifications
'I've got a degree in economics and I'm a member of the Chartered Institute of Marketing.'

Your experience
'I've got 10 years' experience of working in senior roles in sales and marketing in the mobile telecommunications sector.'

Where are you working now?
'I'm currently working as the UK Regional Sales and Marketing Manager with Atlas Telecommunication, based near Farnborough.'

What are you looking for?
'I'm looking for a more challenging role where I can gain some more strategic experience.'

What's your availability and preferred work location?
'I'm available at four weeks' notice and I'm completely flexible on location. I would also relish the opportunity to gain some international experience.'

All of the advice about customising the profile in your CV also applies here. You might want to consider preparing several *different* pitches to cover every eventuality.

A good example would be a **human resources manager** who has both HR generalist skills and also some specialist HR skills in the talent and rewards industry. She might prepare two different pitches, one highlighting her generalist experience and another highlighting her specialist knowledge and experience of talent and rewards.

Here are two examples of pitches for two different senior HR roles. Notice that Angela is closely following the model detailed above.

Angela's HR generalist pitch
'My name is Angela Smith. I'm a very experienced HR manager. I've got a degree in economics from the University of Bristol and I've recently completed an Executive MBA in International HR Management from Cranfield University. I've got 10 years' HR management experience working in the financial services industry. I'm currently working for a large investment bank and I've been based in both their London and New York offices. I'm now looking for a more challenging role where I can apply my knowledge and international experience to a more senior position with responsibility for the entire HR function. I'm

available with 3 months' notice and I am very flexible on my work location, although I have a preference for working in central London.'

Angela's talent management pitch

'My name is Angela Smith. I'm a very experienced talent and rewards specialist. I've got a degree in economics and I've recently completed an Executive MBA in International Human Resources at Cranfield University. During the course I focused on the design of both long- and short-term incentive schemes. I've worked for a major investment bank in the City of London and in New York and I have undertaken a number of key projects where I was able to diagnose and resolve issues relating specifically to talent and rewards through the introduction of enhanced incentive programmes. I'm available with 3 months' notice and I am very flexible on my work location, although I have a preference for working in central London.'

Angela has not invented any of this experience. She has the qualifications and experience required for both jobs. However, because she undertook careful research before making the calls she knew what her contacts were looking for. She changed the focus of her pitch to reflect their actual needs.

Let's look at another example for a less senior role.

Richard Cross has a BSc in Marketing from the University of Leeds and 2 years' work experience in sales with an events business. He spotted a job advertisement on the website of another events company and now has the opportunity to speak to the managing director.

Have a look at the essential requirements for this position as a **marketing assistant** with the events management company.

The successful candidate will:

- have event marketing and delegate acquisition techniques
- have multi-tasking and time management skills
- be highly accurate with great attention to detail
- be target oriented
- have been educated to degree level – marketing-related desirable.

Using the same pitch guidelines, Richard calls the MD and introduces himself.

'My name is Richard Cross. I'm a marketing specialist. I've got a degree in marketing from the University of Leeds and I'm currently studying part time for a postgraduate diploma in marketing with the Chartered Institute of Marketing. I've got 2 years' experience working in the event management business including 6 months working on event marketing and delegate acquisition with a conference organiser in Dubai. I managed to hit all my targets and in fact I received an award from our MD for enrolling the highest number of delegates for last year's UAE medical conference. I'm currently working for Alpha Events and I've been based in both their London and Dubai offices. I'm now looking for a more challenging role with a larger business where I can apply my knowledge and international experience. I'm available with 4 weeks' notice and I am very flexible on my work location; I'm single and I can work anywhere.'

Note how Richard has included his work experience that is relevant to the particular job. Because he carefully prepared his pitch before the call he covered all the key requirements for the job. Assuming that Richard's CV can back up his experience then he's almost certain to get offered an interview.

Making a pitch as a new graduate with little or no work experience

But supposing you are a graduate with little or no work experience? You are chasing that perfect internship that could just get you the opportunity you've been looking for. With no work experience you need to think about other aspects of your experience that may be relevant to the employer. Try to get a clear understanding of what the internship will involve and then try to match the requirement to *any* experience that you may have. Have you travelled abroad? Have you undertaken any voluntary work? Have you organised an event of some kind? Have you had a part-time job? If you have *no* experience of any kind then before applying for an internship my advice would be to go out and get some experience! A part-time job as a shop assistant will give you a great insight into the retail sector, customer service, working as part of a team, sales and so on. Organising a fun run or helping out with a local charity could get you great experience of project management, event management, sales and marketing (even if it's selling tickets to the local summer fete!). Focus on things that really interest you but will also provide you with experience that will be relevant to that pitch for an internship or first job.

Here's an example of the requirements for an internship with an advertising agency.

> An interest in marketing, advertising or public relations. Familiarity with (primarily) PC-based applications such as Microsoft Word, Microsoft Excel, Microsoft PowerPoint, etc. A curious, inquisitive nature and familiarity with sourcing information from the web. Naturally friendly and outgoing; interested in working with people and in a team . . .

A recent graduate, Paula, would like to apply for this position and has the opportunity to speak to the recruitment manager.

'Hello, my name is Paula Taylor and I'm interested in a career in advertising. I've recently graduated from the University of Bradford with a degree in English. I don't have any professional work experience in advertising but at university I was involved in a number of activities where I needed to advertise events and also to promote my own activities when I took part in a half marathon for charity. I've got plenty of experience of using Microsoft Office and I also created posters and advertisements for events at university and I recently created a personal website and used it to promote my half marathon. I'm currently doing some charity work with Cancer Research and I really enjoy working with people from different backgrounds. I could be available at short notice for this opportunity and I'm completely flexible on my work location.'

Note that the same model can be applied to pitches for roles in any job category at any point in your career.

Whatever your experience it will pay you to prepare several different pitches so that, whenever you meet or speak to a new network contact, you can provide a professional and well structured summary of your experience and key skills that will be relevant for that contact based on your research. You do not need to stick rigidly to this model and you certainly don't want to sound too rehearsed; however, in my experience many candidates (including the most senior managers) do not always do themselves justice when asked the simple question 'Tell me about yourself'. Thinking carefully about what the individual contact is looking for and including all the key details of your background will ensure that you make the best possible impression when you speak to a new and potentially important contact.

CHECKLIST FOR YOUR PITCH

Introduce yourself

_____
_____
_____
_____

Your professional role

_____
_____
_____
_____

Your education and qualifications

_____
_____
_____
_____

Your experience

_____
_____
_____
_____

Where are you working now?

_____
_____
_____
_____

What are you looking for?

_____
_____
_____

What's your availability and preferred work location?

_____
_____
_____
_____

TOTAL JOB SEARCH TIP

Tailor your pitch to match the needs of your contact.

Writing an email enquiry to a network contact

If an email or letter seems to be a better way of introducing yourself to a contact then use the same model to write your pitch, and then, if you haven't had a response within 48 hours, follow up with a phone call.

To: richard.small@email.com
From: angela.smith@email.co.uk
Subject: Potential HR opportunities

Dear Richard

Mike Richards at Proctor Financial suggested that I contact you. My name is Angela Smith and I'm writing to enquire if you have any opportunities within your HR department.

I'm a very experienced talent and rewards specialist. I've got a degree in economics and I've recently completed an Executive MBA in International Human Resources at Cranfield University. During the course I focused on the design of both long- and short-term incentive schemes. I've worked for a major investment bank in the City of London and in New York and I have undertaken a number of key projects where I was able to diagnose and resolve issues relating specifically to talent and rewards through the introduction of enhanced incentive programmes. I'm available with 3 months' notice and I am very flexible on my work location, although I have a preference for central London.

Thank you very much for your time and consideration and please do contact me by phone or email if you would like any further information.

Kind regards

Angela Smith
T: 01432 678912

Keep in touch with your contacts!

As you begin to grow your network of contacts you will need to organise them efficiently. One possibility would be a drawer full of business cards (!) but it's probably a better idea to start using the contacts feature on your phone or within Microsoft Outlook to keep a record of all the new contacts that you make. With Microsoft Outlook you have all the tools you need to transfer the information from a business card and also make notes about the conversation you had with a particular contact. If the contact suggested that you 'call back in a couple of weeks' it will be very easy to schedule that call within Outlook. If you don't have access to Microsoft Outlook or a similar application then at least use some simple record cards and a diary to keep contact details and place a reminder in your schedule to call back.

Even if you haven't specifically agreed to call in a couple of weeks, it will still be worth making the *occasional* follow-up call. It often happens that the contact who had nothing for you on the last call would now like to speak to you. This advice is also relevant for your close contacts. Stay in touch with them on a regular basis. Again, they may not have had suitable jobs the last time you called but that may have changed. It may be worth asking if it would be convenient to call back and you certainly don't want to alienate your contact by calling too frequently.

If you are phoning then it is common courtesy to ask if it is a convenient time to call and to offer to call back if necessary. Before making your pitch you will need to introduce yourself and explain the context of your call. For example:

'John Brown [a mutual acquaintance or a previous contact] mentioned that you might be aware of some opportunities within your company. Is now a convenient time to discuss potential jobs?'

When the response to this introduction is positive you can ask further questions to confirm the details of any jobs that might be available. The answers to these questions will then help you to tailor your pitch to suit the requirements.

Once you have completed the call, whatever the outcome, follow up with a polite email to say thank you and to provide any information requested.

Some people find the idea of cold calling very difficult and of course sometimes you will get a negative response from a contact who either can't or won't help. You need to stay positive and move on to the next call. The very worst thing that can happen is that your contact can't help you, and, of course, the very best thing that can happen is that they have inside information about your perfect job.

Other ways to network

Up to now we have discussed what could be described as *active* networking where you go out and actively find new contacts. However, networking is a two-way activity and you can also profitably engage in *passive* networking – that is, making it easier for people to network and find you.

Recruiters are getting more and more imaginative in the methods they use to search for candidates for their clients. Of course, the internet job sites are a massive resource for the recruitment industry, but what other ways are there for you to increase your visibility to recruiters?

Writing a blog

You might consider starting an online blog focused on your area of professional expertise. If you are an experienced **procurement professional** then a blog sharing your experience with other procurement specialists would be a very valuable activity. Setting up a blog is straightforward and anyone who is reasonably computer literate should be able to start a blog using the free resources available from http://wordpress.org or using Google's blogging resource at www.blogger.com.

Starting a blog may not sound like an activity that should come at the top of your list of priorities during your job search but many business professionals blog regularly and, while it may not be your primary job search strategy, it most certainly is a good way to dramatically increase your *visibility* on the internet.

In the context of a job search you should of course use all the appropriate keywords in your blog to ensure that your details will be found by recruiters.

As an experienced recruiter I have, on many occasions, failed to find a candidate with very specific skills by searching the internet job sites; however, by putting my keywords into a search engine such as Google I have found a number of potential candidates in quite different locations on the internet.

A blog can certainly help with your job search and increase your visibility online but be careful what you write. Remember that anything that you write online can be read by anyone searching the web. Writing something negative about your job or criticising your last employer is always going to be a bad idea. Writing something positive, interesting and constructive that illustrates your professional expertise will most definitely be well received.

Your personal 'brand'

Many recruiters and employers enter the names of potential candidates for jobs into a search engine to look for any extra information that would enable them to make a hiring decision. If you don't want everybody to read what you've written then don't post it. Remember that what people read about you on the internet can also have a negative impact on your job search.

For that reason you should start to think about your *personal brand* online. Assuming that recruiters find your details online, how will they perceive you? Will the online content reflect on you positively or not? If there are 'private' areas of your life then make sure that they remain private by using the appropriate permissions on sites such as Facebook. If you intend the online content to be found, then you need to control it. The danger is that the very controlled content of your CV may be undone by the trail of information about you that might be found on the internet. Remember that recruiters and employers *do* enter people's names into Google to check up on a potential candidate. I can think of at least two instances where candidates were on the point of receiving a job offer and then the offers were revoked following an internet search. In one case the candidate's LinkedIn profile indicated that they had omitted a job from their CV and changed the dates to hide the fact that they had worked for a particular company for only 3 months. In the other case the candidate had been indiscreet in allowing the content of their Facebook page to be public.

Regardless of age, regardless of position, regardless of the business we happen to be in, all of us need to understand the importance of branding. We are CEOs of our own companies: Me Inc. To be in business today, our most important job is to be head marketer for the brand called You.

Tom Peters American management guru

Many of us make an excellent job of developing our employer's brand but pay a lot less attention to the most important brand of all – our own personal brand. Enter your own name into a search engine and see what you find. If there is anything that might have a negative impact on your job search then try to find a way to correct it or remove it.

TOTAL JOB SEARCH TIP

Check that any online personal information is positive.

There are other activities that you can undertake that may significantly affect your personal brand. It's well known that recruiters often call people to ask for recommendations or referrals. For example, a recruiter will call a contact and ask if they can recommend someone for a particular job. Could *you* be the person they would recommend?

Become famous

Becoming famous or becoming an acknowledged expert in your particular field is one excellent way to be recommended when the recruiter or headhunter makes that call. So it should also become an important part of your networking activities to make sure that people within your field know that you are available and looking for a new job.

Another way to enhance your personal brand is to undertake a responsible role outside your professional field. Have you considered becoming a committee member or chair of your club or association? Could you become a governor of your children's school? All of these activities are likely to be noted on the internet and will further reinforce your personal brand in a positive way.

Have you considered offering to speak at industry events within your field? Could you write an article for publication in a trade magazine that is going to be read by potential employers? That brilliant new strategy, marketing technique or incentive scheme might just be the spark that leads to a phone call that gets you your next job.

Optimise your LinkedIn profile

As discussed in Chapter 3, LinkedIn (www.linkedin.com) is the professional equivalent of Facebook on the internet. It's an excellent resource which you can use to search for jobs and to research potential contacts.

LinkedIn has around 175 million members worldwide. Recruiters use LinkedIn to search for candidates for jobs in exactly the same way as they search the internet job sites. By optimising your LinkedIn profile you will ensure that recruiters find your details and contact you about job opportunities.

With so many people registered on LinkedIn it's very important to make sure that your profile will stand out from the crowd.

The professional headline
Ideally this should be the job title that most accurately reflects what you do, or better still the job title that you expect recruiters will specify when searching for people with your skills and experience. For example:

Malcolm Craig
ATPL-rated Helicopter Pilot

Here are some further examples providing a little more information to optimise your headline:

- Creative Director and Web Designer
- Oracle HR Implementation Specialist
- Degree-qualified Computer Forensics Expert
- Finance Director – UK-qualified Chartered Accountant
- Public Sector Procurement Specialist
- Java Software Engineer
- Qualified IT Project Manager
- TOGAF-qualified Systems Architect
- Hands-on Retail Manager
- CIPD-qualified HR Manager.

Note that the professional headline can also contain a keyword or phrase that will ensure that your details are found more easily by recruiters. If you are not getting the right responses try using different headlines and keywords to match the words that you expect recruiters to be searching for in your job category.

In this section you can also specify your sector/industry. This is important. Many recruiters will search for candidates with specific industry experience and job advertisements often specify a requirement for previous experience in a particular industry. Choose your industry carefully as you may not be found if your industry selection does not match a particular requirement. If you have worked in the same industry for many years and you wish to continue in the same industry then this will not be a problem. If you have worked in a number of different industries then you will need to use either the industry that you have worked in most recently or the industry that you would like to work in. Consider changing this setting from time to time to see if you get a better response.

Professional experience and goals

The next section covers **professional experience and goals**. You can use a similar format to the profile in your CV to go in this section.

For example:

Java software engineer with a degree in computer studies from the University of Bath and with 18 months' work experience. Currently studying for the ISEB

Foundation Qualification in Software Testing and interested in working for a small software house with responsibility for both coding and testing.

Directly under the summary section is a section for specialties. This is a good place to insert some keywords that you believe recruiters will use to find job seekers with your background.

For example: Java, software, engineer, degree, computer studies, coding, ISEB, testing.

In the experience section you can simply add the career history section of your CV. If you are working for a small company it may be useful to add a brief description of the companies you have been working for.

Note also that LinkedIn permits you to add three hyperlinks to websites. These could include a link to your current employer's website but, even better, could be a link to your personal website or blog. Remember that recruiters will be using LinkedIn not only to find good candidates for their clients but also to research a candidate's background. Of course your profile and career history will be on LinkedIn, but an external link to your blog, perhaps describing a particularly successful project or an interesting or innovative approach, will add depth to your profile and so increase the chances that the recruiter will want to contact you.

Find keywords in job advertisements

You should constantly monitor job advertisements for jobs that you might apply for and make sure that the keywords used are contained both in your CV and in your LinkedIn profile. A good example would be this extract from a recent advertisement on LinkedIn for a **sales manager**.

- A **team player** mentality with a record of successful sales management in the UK **travel industry**.
- Ideally 8–15 years' experience in **sales, account management** or **partner-relationship management** roles.

- A robust network of **UK industry contacts**, ensuring expedient development of a high-quality merchant pipeline.
- Excellent **prospecting** and **negotiating** skills and an ability to articulate **sales propositions** clearly and appropriately based on audience.
- Innovative, team-oriented and collaborative, and able to multi-task and prioritise effectively in a fast-paced environment where priorities change quickly.

Notice that I have highlighted a number of keywords in this advertisement. As a sales manager these are the words and phrases that are going to appear again and again in job advertisements for sales roles. They are also words and phrases that a recruiter will use to search for candidates for their clients. The recruiter for this particular role might very well put into their LinkedIn search the following string using the Boolean technique:

'Sales manager' AND 'travel industry' AND 'account management' AND negotiating AND 'team player'

This kind of search is employed by thousands of recruiters every day. If your CV or LinkedIn profile does not contain those keywords it will not be found. Make sure that you use the keywords that recruiters will be using to find people like you.

We've already seen that LinkedIn is a very useful resource where you can search for jobs, network and make contact with fellow professionals. You can also use LinkedIn as part of your research prior to an interview. Let's assume that you have been invited to an interview with a company. Use the search facility on LinkedIn to find the names and backgrounds of the people who work there. Are you looking for the name of the IT director? Have a look on LinkedIn – it will be useful to know where they worked previously. Perhaps you once worked for the same company or worked in the same market. This is all vital information that will help you prepare for your interview. You may even discover the name of someone you know who is currently working for the same company. Get in touch to find out as much as you can about the organisation before your interview.

Of course, you can also use LinkedIn to build your network of contacts. Send an invitation to connect via LinkedIn to build connections with people who may be able to help you with your job search. For a reasonable subscription you can upgrade from the free 'Basic' account on LinkedIn to a 'Business Plus' account (approximately £30 a month); this will enable you to contact a larger number of contacts via LinkedIn *In Mail*. There's no contract and this would be an excellent investment in return for access to the 175 million professionals registered on LinkedIn.

IN A NUTSHELL

- Build up a list of both close contacts and acquaintances.
- Try to get referrals from your first line of contacts.
- Don't waste an opportunity when speaking to a new contact – develop your elevator pitch.
- Consider using a script (or at least detailed notes) to make sure that you mention all of your unique selling points.
- Research your contacts and then tailor your pitch to their needs and expectations.
- Think about passive networking and build your own online brand.
- Be careful of the footprint you leave on the internet – keep your personal life private.
- Consider writing a professional blog and use the right keywords to attract new readers.
- If you are not already on LinkedIn then consider registering now.
- Optimise your LinkedIn profile to use the right job title, keywords and industry.

5 THE JOB APPLICATION

We now come to a critical stage of your job search campaign, the job application. Your application can take several different forms, including the traditional letter and printed CV, online applications or applications by email. Increasingly employers are also asking candidates to complete application forms either in hard copy or electronically. And then there is the issue of the application (or covering) letter, which may be the very first item that a recruiter sees before reading your CV or application form. Making sure that your application stands out from the crowd and clearly demonstrates that you have all the required skills and experience for the job is the subject of this chapter.

This chapter will help you:

■ understand the requirements of the different types of job application

- write a compelling job application letter or email that will ensure that you get shortlisted for interview

- write speculative job application letters or emails

- complete job application forms

- answer competency questions on application forms.

You've created an excellent CV, you've searched for jobs on the internet and in the press and you've now identified a job or jobs that you would like to apply for. Applying for jobs on internet job sites could not be easier and you could in theory make multiple job applications in minutes. If the jobs exactly match your skills, experience and qualifications and your CV clearly provides evidence of your fit for the jobs then this approach is fine. However, it is more likely that you will want to make some adjustments to your CV as suggested in Chapter 2. In fact, my advice would be to customise your CV for each and every job application. Bear in mind that the majority of the applicants for a particular job will have simply sent off the same CV and standard covering letter for every job. If you want your application to stand out from the crowd then you need to do more. As suggested earlier you should first ensure that the requirements, as set out in the job advertisement, are clearly reflected in your CV. Make any necessary changes and also consider underlining particularly relevant skills or experience or putting them in bold type.

Remember also to make sure that your CV is in a format that will be retained when you send it through to the recruiter. A Microsoft Word document is the standard format used throughout the recruitment industry worldwide. However, even within Word there can be formatting issues. The only certain way to ensure that your CV is properly formatted is to send it as a PDF document. This will guarantee the proper formatting and also ensure that the document cannot be altered in any way. As previously stated there are a number of free applications available on the internet that will enable you to convert your standard Word document to the PDF format.

Your CV is just one part of your job application. The next important element is your covering letter. The style of this document will vary depending on the types of application that you are making.

These might include:

■ applications made via an internet job site
■ applications by email
■ applications by post.

Job applications made via a job site

If you have registered with a job site you have probably already uploaded your CV to the site. You may have had the option to upload several different versions of your CV and you can complete a covering letter that will be sent along with your CV. Be careful to check that you are not applying for the same job several times. Many employers use a number of different agencies to search for candidates for their jobs. Carefully compare the wording of any advertisements before making an application. If in doubt call the agency concerned to confirm details before sending off multiple applications. If the employer receives several applications from the same candidate through different agencies this may send out the wrong message.

Job applications by email

Very often if you see a job advertised in a newspaper or on a job site you will be invited to apply for the job by email. One important factor would be how you send your covering letter. My advice would be to send both your CV and the covering letter as separate attachments. Email formatting can look very untidy and your carefully composed and formatted covering letter could finish up looking a mess on the recipient's screen. You should also use a sensible subject line in your email. Read the job advertisement carefully as sometimes the advertiser will specify the format of the subject line for email applications. Otherwise I would recommend using the format on the following page.

From: colin.jones@email.com
To: richard.oldman@email.com
Subject: Application for the position of Project Manager
(Ref: 12345/6)

Richard

I am writing with reference to the position of Project Manager which was advertised in *Computer Weekly* on Thursday 20th September. I am extremely interested in this position and I believe that I have all the required skills and experience to succeed in this important role.

As you will see from my CV (attached) I am a very experienced project manager with a strong track record of effectively delivering projects throughout my career. I have first-hand experience of managing the delivery of complex, high-value mobile software solutions to enterprise customers in both the UK and Europe.

I have excellent communication and interpersonal skills with a proven ability to quickly win the trust and respect of others. I currently manage a team of 10 software specialists with my current employer, Eagle Communications, based in London.

I have a BSc (Hons) in Computer Science and Telecommunications (2:i) from the University of Bedford.

I am available for interview at your convenience. Please do call me if you require any further information or if you would like to arrange a meeting.

Regards

Colin Jones
Tel: 01234 567890

General guidelines for job applications

Every job application needs to be treated with a great deal of attention to detail. The job application is full of traps for the unwary. I have received so many job applications (often from very senior executives) that just had to go straight in the bin. One candidate applied for a job in financial services with a lengthy paragraph about their strengths in sales and marketing in the telecommunications sector. Another (clearly confused candidate!) sent in an application explaining at length why they wanted to work for the company's main competitor. By far the biggest cause for rejection of job applications is the presence of spelling and grammar mistakes. This is probably the biggest concern of recruiters and practically guarantees that your application will not be considered. Don't just rely on your spellchecker. Read and re-read your CV and covering letter and then get a friend or relative to check it as well.

Basic format of the application letter

Writing an application letter (or covering letter) may seem to be difficult, particularly if you have to write a specific letter for each application. However, if you follow a few basic guidelines you will find that it is not quite so bad.

It is generally expected that you will send some kind of covering letter with every job application. It is extremely important to pay attention to writing a carefully constructed covering letter each time you apply for a job; it could make the difference between being invited for interview and being rejected. Ideally the covering letter should complement your CV and its purpose is to highlight the skills and experience that you have that match the requirements of the job as described in the job advertisement or job specification. Your application letter may be the very first contact that you have with your potential employer so it's very important to get it right and to make a good first impression.

Apart from the different methods of application that we have already mentioned there are two types of covering letter:

- a covering letter for a specific advertised vacancy
- a speculative application letter enquiring about a *possible* vacancy.

An effective application letter should set out why you are interested in the organisation you are applying to and also highlights how you match the requirements of the job.

Here's a suggested format for an application letter.

First paragraph

Explain why you are writing and confirm the job that you are applying for and the job reference (if available). You may also want to indicate where and when you saw the job advertised.

Second paragraph

Describe the specific skills and experience that you have. Try to highlight the specific skills and experience that match the requirements set out in the job advertisement.

Third paragraph

Describe some of your personal qualities that would make you a suitable candidate for the job.

Fourth paragraph

Highlight any qualifications or training that are either requested in the job advertisement or would be relevant to the job that you are applying for.

Final paragraph

Write a concluding paragraph emphasising your enthusiasm for the job and repeating that you are a good match for the job described in the advertisement.

Close and signature

For an email it is generally best to use 'Regards'. You can write your full name (i.e. John Brown) and you might also wish to add your telephone number or email address to make it even easier for a recruiter to contact you.

For a letter, you should use either 'Yours sincerely' if writing to someone by name or 'Yours faithfully' if you begin the letter with 'Dear Sir or Madam'.

John Brown
128 London Road
Reading
Berkshire
RG40 4RA

Richard Ingram
Recruitment Director
Park Technologies
Centaur Business Park
Slough
Berkshire
AN56 8HU

21 March 2012

Dear Mr Ingram

Head of Talent – Ref: ABC/1234

I have enclosed my CV in response to your advertisement for the position of Head of Talent (Ref: ABC/1234) which was advertised in *The Sunday Times* last weekend.

As you will see from my CV I have specific expertise in the design and implementation of a talent management strategy that is aligned to the need for sales growth. I have recently completed a project to assess high leadership potential amongst our sales and marketing managers and I implemented a specific talent management strategy designed to increase sales and improve staff retention.

I have over 10 years' experience in talent management and I also have very good generalist HR experience. I have undertaken a number of projects where I was able to analyse and resolve issues related to talent.

I have a BA in Modern Languages (2:i) from Bristol University and I have recently completed an MBA in International Human Resources at Cranfield University. I speak French and German fluently.

I believe that my professional experience would provide an excellent basis for success in this role and I hope that you will look favourably on my application. Thank you for your time and consideration and I look forward to hearing from you in due course.

Yours sincerely

John Brown
Tel: 01234 567891

Speculative letters

In some cases you may be writing a speculative letter where you are enquiring about possible opportunities with an employer. In this case you need to state your specific objective and describe the kind of job that you are looking for and why you have decided to apply to this particular organisation. Since this is an unsolicited letter it is even more important to make a strong first impression otherwise it may not be read. See the example over the page.

Richard Tate
23 Mayfield Drive
Rudwell
West Sussex
BN19 9RA

Mike Fleming
Chief Technology Officer
Tate Software
Unit 20
West Park Business Centre
Windsor
Berkshire
RG34 7YU

21 March 2012

Dear Mr Fleming

I am writing to enquire if you have a vacancy for a computer security specialist within your IT department.

I have a First Class Honours degree in Computer Science from the University of Bedford and I have recently completed an MSc in Computer Security and Forensics from the University of Holloway. I have 18 months' IT experience gained primarily within the oil and gas industry.

I understand that your company produces software for the oil and gas industry and I believe that my industry knowledge plus my expertise in IT security would be of value to Tate Software.

I have enclosed my CV for your reference and I would appreciate it if you would let me know if you might have a suitable vacancy.

Thank you very much for your time and please do call me if you require any further information.

Yours sincerely

Richard Tate
T: 01234 567891
E: richard.tate@email.com

Completing application forms

Some employers now ask you to apply for a job using an application form. The reason that they do this is so that they can compare all the candidates who apply for the job or jobs on an equal basis.

If you receive a copy of the application form in the post and you need to complete it by hand it is a good idea to make a photocopy (or photocopies) so that you can practise writing your answers to the questions on the form. If it is an online application then download several copies. Again, this is so that you can practise your responses several times before completing the form that you will post off to the employer. If the form can be completed from your computer then this is always preferable but there are still quite a large number of employers who require job applicants to complete forms by hand. You should always keep copies of your applications so that you have a complete record of exactly what information you sent to each employer. If for any reason your application is not successful, ask for feedback so that you can use the information to improve the quality of your applications in the future.

Organisations that request a completed job application form generally also include a job specification and detailed instructions on how to complete the form and what kind of answers are expected. Be sure to read the instructions very carefully as employers may be very strict in assessing your application. Any mistakes or incorrect answers may mean that your application will not be considered.

The different sections of an application form

Very often the first section of the application form will request your **personal details**. These may be marked confidential and can be separated from the main application before shortlisting takes place. This format is very much to your advantage as it means that the information contained in the main application form will be screened entirely on your experience and without any reference to your name, age or gender. Furthermore, if you have a medical condition or disability this information will also not be available to the reviewer. Many employers are now adopting this fairer and more objective screening process.

PERSONAL DETAILS – CONFIDENTIAL

Please complete this form using black ink or type. This form is separated from your application before shortlisting takes place. It is not used at any stage of the selection process.

Post title: Finance Director	**Reference:** ABC/1234
Where did you see this post advertised?	The Sunday Times
PERSONAL DETAILS	
Last name: Green	**First name(s):** Richard
Address:	**Known as:**
128 Reading Lane	**Title e.g. Mr/Mrs:** Mr
Reading	**Previous last name(s):**
Postcode: RG90 4XX	**Email address:** richard.green@ email.com
Preferred contact no.: 01234 567891	**Date of birth:** 03/07/70
DFE no. (if applicable): N/A	**NI number:** V123456Z
Are you able to work lawfully in the UK?	YES
Do you consider yourself to have a disability, learning difficulty or long-term medical condition?	NO
Do you have any requirements that will help you with an interview (such as an accessible interview room, hearing loop)?	NO
If yes, please specify requirements:	N/A

APPLICATION FOR EMPLOYMENT

Please complete in black ink or type.

Post title: Finance Director	**Reference:** ABC/1234
Last name: Green	**First name:** Richard
PRESENT/MOST RECENT EMPLOYMENT (if applicable)	
Name of employer: Paper Company Limited	
Address of employer: Unit 1, Salway Business Park, West Sendon, Berkshire RG5 5TH	
Position held: Finance Director	
Start date: May 2007	**Date of leaving:** N/A
Reason for leaving (if applicable): Looking for a more challenging role with a larger company.	
Hours of work: 40 hours	**Salary:** £75,000 + bonus/ benefits including company car

Present and previous employment

You will need to provide details of your present and previous employment in this section. Generally there is space for quite a lot of detail about this. Take the bullets that you placed in the **career history** section of your CV and convert them into sentences that can be read as one or two paragraphs. In this example Richard Green's career history for his most recent job reads as follows.

- Built strong relationships with senior stakeholders and developed excellent working relationships with clients.
- Supported the business in the preparation of budgets and forecasts.
- Reduced operating costs by 25% following a review of existing service agreements.
- Delivered comprehensive monthly and annual reporting to provide accurate financial/management information.
- Undertook a successful change management project following the acquisition of another business.
- Demonstrated good team-building skills and increased the finance team from 10 to 20 staff.

Note how these bullets have been converted into a more suitable style for the application form (as shown below).

Brief description of duties and responsibilities:

In my most recent role I built strong relationships with senior stakeholders and developed excellent working relationships with our clients. I supported the business in the preparation of budgets and forecasts and reduced operating costs by 25% following a review of existing service agreements. I delivered comprehensive monthly and annual reporting to provide accurate financial/management information. I also undertook a successful change management project following the acquisition of another business.

I believe that I demonstrated good team-building skills and I increased the finance team from 10 to 20 staff over a period of 5 years.

Prior to your most recent employment, you may be required to simply provide dates, employer name and position for earlier jobs (see example on the next page). As we discussed in Chapter 2, it's important not to leave any gaps in your employment history; so if for any reason you were not working for a period of time, be sure to show what you were doing and do not be tempted to modify dates to cover up any employment gaps. You should list your experience in date order with your most recent job first. You may also be asked to provide a reason for leaving. Try to use very positive language here to emphasise that you left because you were looking for improved prospects, greater responsibility and better opportunities for promotion.

If you are a recent graduate or school leaver and you do not have any work experience then of course you can leave this section blank; however, do add details of any part-time work or vacation jobs that you might have undertaken.

EMPLOYMENT

List in date order with the most recent first, stating whether the employment was full time (F) or part time (P). Include dates of employment and reasons for any break in employment. Please continue on a separate sheet if necessary.

From	To	Employer	Position	Full/part time	Reason for leaving
05/04	04/07	Proctor Ltd	Head of Finance	F	Improved prospects
02/01	04/01	Parkers Ltd	Chief Accountant	F	Opportunity for promotion

Competency-based questions on application forms

On some application forms you may find competency-based questions that you will need to answer. These may be closed questions that ask for some specific information but very often they are questions that are based on the requirements of the job and require you to draw on your personal experience. You will often need to answer the question using a limited number of words, so you need to give a succinct but comprehensive response.

Using the **STAR** acronym (Situation, Task, Action, Result) will help you to keep on track and provide the answer in a structured format.

EXPERIENCE, KNOWLEDGE, SKILLS, COMPETENCIES AND ATTRIBUTES

Please give details of why you are applying for this post and how you meet the requirements set out in the person specification.

Reducing costs

At the Paper Company Limited the supplier agreements had not been reviewed for a number of years. I was tasked with reducing costs on existing supplier agreements. I set up a competitive tender with a number of suppliers to provide core services including mobile telephony, IT service management and vehicle leasing. I evaluated the supplier proposals and negotiated new contracts. My actions resulted in average cost savings of 25% accompanied by significantly improved levels of service.

Outsourcing

Following an in-depth review, I made the decision to outsource the finance function in some countries and expanded the roles of some of the UK team to focus on European operations. I reduced headcount within the European finance team from 21 to 11 people. As a result, I significantly improved management information across the whole business.

Handling difficult situations

When I was working as an intern at Barclays Bank I became aware of a serious issue with duplicate data held on the bank's database. This meant that, in some cases, customers were receiving incorrect statements or duplicate statements from the bank. The difficulty was that this error should have been spotted by my supervisor. I decided to raise the issue directly with the supervisor. We then worked jointly on providing a solution to quickly rectify the problem. As it turned out, my supervisor was grateful for my intervention and I subsequently received a written commendation from the manager of the department.

TOTAL JOB SEARCH TIP

Use STAR to answer competency questions on application forms.

Interests and achievements

If you don't have much (or any) work experience then this section is particularly important. Try to highlight interests and achievements that will be meaningful to the employer – for example, if you have travelled extensively or if you have good IT skills.

Sometimes you may need to think carefully about some of the activities from your personal life or from your time at university to establish some relevant achievements.

For example:

- organised a large social function for my university Students' Union
- captained the university football team
- achieved 2:i university degree
- raised £1,000 by completing a charity marathon.

Writing personal statements

Some employers require you to write a personal statement when filling out the job application form. They may ask you to explain why you are applying for the job or why you believe that you are a suitable candidate for the job. They will probably also ask you to provide further details of your skills and experience and any qualifications that are relevant. For school leavers and graduates (with limited work experience) they may also ask for details of your personal interests and achievements.

General guidelines for writing a personal statement

Explain *why* you are applying for this particular job. If you are going to mention personal interests and hobbies then try to link them to the skills and experience required for the job. For example, being captain of your university football team suggests that you have good leadership skills. Organising a large social function would be good evidence of your organisational and project management skills. Bear in mind that your personal statement will almost certainly be used as the basis for a job interview, so be prepared to answer questions about the points that you made. Get the grammar, spelling and punctuation right.

Here's a checklist for the preparation of a personal statement that is often given to students applying for a place at university but could equally apply to job hunters.

- Research/think.
- Plan, perhaps using a mind map or similar technique.
- Write the first draft.
- Check your grammar and spelling.
- Use your spellchecker.
- Print out and leave overnight and then check again.
- Write the final version of the personal statement.
- Final proofread before submitting.

This checklist is an indication of the care and attention that some candidates give to writing a personal statement. Don't be one of the candidates who sends off a hastily written personal statement. This may be one of the key elements of your job application that will decide whether you will be invited to interview or not. If you really want the job then you cannot be too thorough.

Writing a personal statement is not something that you would generally do so it is worth taking some time to practise. Before starting to write, at the planning stage, you may find it helpful to use a mind map (or similar brainstorming technique) to map out all of the points that you want to cover and decide which points best match the requirements of the job. Be aware that many organisations now use sophisticated 'similarity detection' software to detect personal statements that have been copied from documents on the internet. Don't be tempted to copy; you will almost certainly get disqualified from the application process.

Be sure to read the instructions on the application form very carefully so that you address *all* the points mentioned in the job specification and summarise how your skills and experience match the requirements of the job.

Carefully check your application form

Before you send off the application form make sure that you check it carefully and ideally ask a friend or colleague to check it for any mistakes and to ensure that you have answered all the questions and have provided all the required information. Keep a copy of your application and job advertisement details in case you need them for interview preparation.

What to include with your application

You may want to include a number of documents to support your job application. For example:

■ copies of qualifications/certificates
■ references or testimonials.

References may take the form of an actual reference letter or alternatively may be the name and contact details of someone who will provide a reference for you. Remember to check with that individual that they are happy for you to give their name as a referee and that they will be available. Ask them how they would like to be contacted, i.e. by post, email or phone.

Following up on your application

Once you have submitted your job application you may wish to follow up to ensure that your application has been received. You can do this by email or phone; of course, this may also present an opportunity for you to find out more about the job and if you are likely to be selected for interview. It is often the case that candidates who follow up their applications rather than sitting at home waiting for the phone to ring are more successful in their job search. I have experienced this several times, where I was about to reject a candidate when they called me. When I indicated that I was not planning to shortlist the candidate and explained why, it was sometimes the case that I had missed an important point in their application or the candidate was able to convince me that they did in fact have the required experience. The fact that I had not been convinced initially probably suggests that the application could have been better. Nevertheless, if you are very confident that you do have all of the required skills and experience for a particular job then don't hang back – call the recruiter or employer and convince them. A job application is not the time for false modesty – go for it!

Occasionally job advertisements may indicate that only successful candidates will be contacted but I strongly recommend that you do follow up every application whether it is to a recruitment agency or to the employer directly. If the application is to a recruitment agency, offer to explain why you believe that you are well qualified for the job and, if appropriate, offer to go in for a meeting.

TOTAL JOB SEARCH TIP

Get a friend or colleague to check your application for typos and spelling mistakes.

IN A NUTSHELL

- Customise every job application.
- Consider making fewer job applications and focus on jobs where you have all the required skills and experience.
- Don't send out the same CV for every job application; tailor your CV for each one.
- Take equal care with your job applications whether applying from a job site or by regular mail.
- Carefully read through the instructions for completing application forms.
- Make sure that you answer every question in an application form.
- Take care when completing application forms; they may carry more weight than your CV.
- Use the STAR model to structure paragraphs summarising your experience in a particular area.
- Thoroughly check your applications and consider getting a friend or colleague to check for you.
- Do follow up your application. Make sure that it has been received and be prepared to explain why you believe that you are the best candidate for the job.

6 INTERVIEWS

We now come to the most critical phase of your job search. You have done well to have come this far; to the point where an employer believes that you are potentially the right candidate for the job. Your CV and job application have impressed and you are now one of the select few candidates shortlisted for interview. And yet so many candidates throw away this opportunity by not preparing sufficiently. It's no longer possible to just 'hope for the best' on the day. If you are serious about getting a job offer then you need to start preparing well in advance of the interview date and be fully prepared for both the interview format and likely interview questions.

This chapter will help you:

■ prepare thoroughly for your job interview

■ prepare for the different interview formats and different types of interview questions

- anticipate the likely interview questions for a particular job and then practise your responses

- recognise and answer competency-based interview questions using an easily learned technique

- plan and ask your own questions at the interview.

General guidelines for interview preparation

Success at job interviews comes from a combination of factors which ensure that potential employers see you at your best on the day of the interview. Assuming that you have the right skills and experience and you do well at the interview then you have every chance of being offered the job. However, there is nothing more frustrating than walking out of an interview knowing that you could have done much better or that you answered a particular question or series of questions badly or incorrectly. Preparation is the key to interview success and if you do your research and know what to expect you will find that your job interview will be an enjoyable experience and you will increase your chances of success.

There are a number of basics that you need to address before every interview.

Location and time

Get clear and precise details of the location and time of the interview. It is astonishing how many candidates either arrive at the wrong location or arrive late for an interview. Your interviewer(s) will almost certainly be working to a tight schedule and if you arrive 15 minutes late then you will probably have 15 minutes less time than you had expected. Avoid this by checking the location and if necessary doing a dry run *at the time of the interview* so that you are sure that you know how long the journey will take. Aim to arrive at least 15 minutes before the appointed time.

Dress for success

This might seem obvious but, surprisingly, not all candidates for job interviews seem to think it is important. My advice is clear: always dress as smartly as possible for a job interview. Even if you are going to see a recruitment agency rather than the actual employer, make sure you look your best.

There are some subtle variations on the 'dress smart' advice and, of course, there are some business sectors where a business suit might be considered inappropriate. A good tip would be to look on the company website. Are there any photos of staff working there? Try to fit in with whatever seems right for that particular organisation. If you are going through a recruitment agency then ask the advice of the recruitment consultant, who will probably have attended a meeting there. Even if the dress code is 'smart casual' the word 'smart' still applies and turning up for a job interview in scruffy jeans and an unironed T-shirt is never going to be a good idea. You need to look smart and professional at *every* interview.

Personal hygiene

This is a tricky issue but it needs to be mentioned. Attend to your personal hygiene before an interview and don't be tempted to have a last smoke before the interview or, even worse, a quick pint of beer. The smell of cigarettes or alcohol will definitely be considered a negative point by most interviewers.

Understanding the job

The best way to gain an initial understanding of the job is to carefully read and re-read the job specification or job advertisement. If you have applied for the job through a recruitment agency they should also provide you with a thorough briefing on the role.

Remember that sometimes the actual job can be very different to the job specification. If you are not applying through a recruitment agency, look at the company website and read the trade press to try and find out a little more about the job that you are applying for.

Prepare your own interview

Many candidates for jobs (particularly for senior roles) are themselves experienced interviewers. In that case prepare an interview for a candidate for the job you have applied for. Write down the questions and think carefully about what answers you would expect to hear.

Research the employer

Plan to spend *at least* 2 hours researching the organisation. Don't leave this until the morning of the interview.

As a minimum you should have answers to these questions.

- Who is the chief executive or managing director?
- When was the organisation founded?
- What are their key products or services?
- Who are their major competitors?
- How are they performing financially?

All of this information will help you to build up a clearer picture of the background to the job that you are applying for. Don't get caught out by the very first question at many interviews: *'What do you know about us?'* Demonstrate that you have done your research thoroughly by giving a very well thought-out response and make it clear *why* you would like to work for that particular organisation. Look at the company website, find their annual report (if available) and use a search engine such as Google to find out as much as you can before the interview. Perhaps you have a friend or relative who works for the organisation or has done business with them. Ask them if they can provide you with any additional background and use this information to prepare some of your own questions for the interview.

Research the interviewer or interviewers

If you know the name(s) of the interviewer(s) try to find out as much as you can about them. Try putting their names into a search engine (or search LinkedIn) and see if you can find their biography on the company website. It's important that you know about the person you are seeing for a number of reasons. For example, if you are attending an interview for a technical role (perhaps in information technology or engineering) and your first interview is with the HR manager then you might expect that the questions at that interview will focus mainly on you as an individual and not on your technical expertise. If, on the other hand, the interviewer is the IT director or head of engineering then you can expect a different line of questioning.

Different types of interview

There are several different types of job interview and you should be aware of these as your preparation for each will need to be different. The interview type may affect the actual format of the interview and the types of questions that you will be asked.

Recruitment agency interviews

You should treat the recruitment agency interview just as seriously as you would an interview with an employer. Your experience (as shown on your CV) must have impressed the agency recruiter; however, they have a duty to submit only the very best or most suitable candidates to the employer. Make sure that the recruitment consultant can see how keen you are on the job and dress and present yourself exactly as you would for the employer interview. Remember that the recruiter may be interviewing quite a number of candidates before making a final shortlist for submission to the employer.

One further feature of the agency interview is the amount of extra information that the recruiter can give you. Use the agency interview as a key element in your preparation for the interview with the employer.

The traditional interview

Many employers still carry out relatively unstructured 'traditional' interviews. The questions asked will depend, to a certain extent, on the type of job and the individual candidate. The interviewer will typically want to explore your background and perhaps your reasons for applying for a particular job. The interviewer will also want to confirm the details of your career to date and your qualifications as shown on your CV. Make sure that you are clear on the dates of your employment and the details of your qualifications; you might consider taking your original qualifications with you to show the interviewer. Be prepared for questions that relate to your motivation for joining a particular employer or for leaving a job. You may also be questioned about key events in your career and your specific achievements in a particular role. If this is your first job or you are at an early stage in your career then the interviewer may also ask about key events in your personal life, perhaps during your time at school or university, or about any voluntary or charity work that you might have undertaken. As suggested in Chapter 2, if you are in the early stages of your career, always try to relate any personal experiences to the requirements of the job. Organising a social function at university or doing a part-time job at the weekends would be good examples of personal experiences that would be relevant and of interest to a potential employer.

In addition to the questions about your background, you can also expect a number of other questions that frequently come up at traditional interviews. Some examples are given below.

'Why do you want to work for us?'

Here is an opportunity for you to demonstrate your knowledge of the employer's business. You might want to begin by outlining some of your achievements in your current role and explain why you now want to change jobs. Perhaps you can't see any further opportunities for promotion or any way to progress in your current role. Perhaps the employer's business offers a more extensive range of products or services than your current employer.

Whatever your response, you must have a well thought-out reason for wanting the job. If you are a graduate or school leaver with limited work experience then use your life experience and other non-work-related achievements and emphasise how these achievements fit in with the requirements of the job. For example, if the job calls for someone with strong customer service skills then perhaps you could relate this to a holiday job working in a shop or bar. If organisational skills are required then think of events that you might have organised at school or university.

'Why should we offer you the job?'

Think back to the job description and then take each item one at a time. Work through the job specification pointing out that you have the required qualifications and experience. Where appropriate provide examples of some of your achievements that match the role. For example:

'You asked for candidates with good experience of business development. In my current job I've increased sales from an average of £25,000 per month to over £50,000. I've done that through a combination of hard work and winning new accounts. I've been nominated salesman of the month twice in the last 6 months.'

'How will you add value to our business?'

Again, you can demonstrate your knowledge of the business and perhaps find areas where your experience will count. For example:

'I notice from your website that you've recently started doing business in France. I speak French fluently and I believe that this would be a real asset to your business.'

An alternative would be:

'I've recently completed my MBA in International Human Resources. I notice that you are expanding your business internationally and I believe that my knowledge and training in international HR would enable me to really add value when you are transferring your staff overseas or negotiating overseas employment contracts.'

'What are your key strengths?'

This is a difficult question to answer, particularly if you happen to be British! But a job interview is not the place for false modesty. Go ahead and spell out your key strengths. For example:

'I've got a good degree in IT from the University of Greenwich. On my degree course I specialised in computer forensics which I believe is a key requirement of this job. I'm currently taking another course in software testing which I

think will also be a major asset. In my last job I was able to use my strengths in problems analysis to discover a major flaw in our billing system and my solution saved the business over £50,000 in lost revenue. Finally, I'm a really good team player and I enjoy working with colleagues and constantly developing new skills. I'm a very quick learner.'

'What are your weaknesses?'

A very difficult question to answer. Everybody has weaknesses and I can recall one candidate who answered this question by saying that he 'didn't have any weaknesses' being turned down for a senior job. Much better to own up to some weaknesses, but make sure they are 'good' ones!

For example:

'I have a sharp eye for detail and a tendency to try and do too much myself. I've recently completed a two-day course on delegation and this has really helped me to let go of some of my responsibilities and trust colleagues and members of my team to take on more of the workload.'

Notice how in this answer the candidate has admitted to a weakness but has recognised it and has already taken steps to remedy the problem by attending a course in delegation. Always try to use this model to answer this type of question. Admit to a weakness but make it clear that you are taking steps to rectify the problem.

Competency or behavioural interviews

Many employers are now starting to train their managers in the most effective interview techniques; the 'competency' or 'behavioural' interview is by far the most prevalent.

Competency-based interviewing is an interview technique based on the premise that the best predictor of future behaviour is an analysis of **past behaviour**. It is designed to provide precise information about the applicant's skills, competencies and motives so that interviewers can find a 'best fit' for any given position based on the success factors it requires.

Competency-based interviews are very good news for the candidate. At least you know that the employer has thought carefully about the requirements for the position and has designed questions to thoughtfully probe skills and experience to find the candidate who is the best fit for the job. So much better than the scenario where an untrained interviewer grabs your CV minutes before the interview and makes up the interview questions during the interview. The huge advantage of the competency-based interview for both candidate and employer is that it is fair. All the candidates for a particular job get asked the same set of questions and the final decision will be completely objective and based on clearly defined criteria.

What are competencies?

Before we get to the actual questions and answers it would be good to know precisely what we mean by a competency.

Competencies are defined by the Chartered Institute of Personnel and Development as:

'. . . the behaviours (and where appropriate the technical skills) that individuals must have, or must acquire, to perform effectively at work . . .'

Employers (or more likely their HR departments) develop a **competency framework** for specific types of jobs within their organisation. They use questionnaires, interviews and observation to draw up a list of key competencies that would be essential for someone to perform well in a particular role.

If we take the example of an air traffic controller, the six key competencies that have been identified as being highly predictive of effective performance are the following.

1. Being decisive.
2. Having confidence in dealing with others.
3. Being inclined to follow a set of rules.
4. Being conscious of detail and being accurate.
5. Being relaxed.
6. Basing decisions on data.

The example of an air traffic controller is a good one because the competencies are quite clear-cut. You would definitely not want to employ an indecisive air traffic controller who tended to follow their own set of rules!

For the air traffic controller position, interviewers would draw up a series of questions to probe the candidates' past behaviour in each of these areas.

Of course, the ability to perform effectively in any given job will require a combination of personal behaviours *and* technical skills. For example, air traffic controllers, pilots, engineers and doctors all require many years of training to acquire specific technical skills to perform their jobs effectively, but their personal behaviours are also critical factors in their performance at work. It is relatively easy to ascertain a candidate's technical capabilities but rather more complex to establish if an individual has the right personal behaviours to perform effectively at work.

CASE STUDY: IT PROJECT MANAGER

A good example of this would be the case of an IT project manager. He was technically extremely capable, he had a bachelor's and master's degree in computer science and he had reached his current position on the back of his technical expertise, initially as a brilliant and innovative software engineer and latterly as a technical project manager rolling out complex IT solutions within a large global organisation. He now wanted to take his career to the next level as the chief information officer of a telecommunications business. Up to now he had managed to succeed because of his outstanding technical abilities. But his new role required personal behaviours that he did not have. He was a poor communicator who hated (and feared) speaking in public, and he was a poor networker who tended to be happiest working with a small group of colleagues who shared his technical abilities. Finally, his focus was very much on the technical side of his role; he did not have a corporate vision that would enable him to look at issues from a very broad perspective beyond the IT function and across different departments of the business.

The case study illustrates that while individuals may have the technical skills to perform a particular job, if they don't also have the required personal attributes they will not succeed. Of course, it is possible that people can recognise this shortfall and take steps to improve. In the example above the IT project manager attended a number of courses in public speaking and presentation skills to improve his ability to communicate effectively and then went on to succeed in the more senior position as chief information officer.

You will often find that the competencies required for a particular role are actually listed in the job advertisement or job specification.

A recent advertisement for the HR manager of a leading charity listed the following competencies:

- vision/strategic thinking
- decision-making
- managing the business
- innovation
- leadership
- communication.

Looking at the competencies listed in this advertisement will provide you with a clear indication of the likely line of questioning at interviews for this role.

Remember that competency questions focus on examples of your past behaviour.

Recognising competency questions

If you haven't experienced a competency-based interview before then it would be helpful to be able to recognise a competency question when it comes. Competency questions very typically begin with open questions:

'Can you tell me about a time . . .'
'Can you give an example . . .'
'Can we discuss . . .'
'Can you illustrate . . .'

And so on.

Answering competency questions using STAR

Fortunately we already have the framework in place that will help you answer competency questions in a form that will work well for the interviewer – the **STAR** technique that we used previously when writing up the achievements in your CV (where **S** = Situation, **T** = Task, **A** = Action, **R** = Result).

Remember that competency questions are always about your past experience so the expectation from the interviewer is that you will provide an example of how you managed a particular situation *in the past*.

The interviewer wants you to provide an example from your past experience that will illustrate how you behaved in a certain situation. The trained competency interviewer will be looking for a 'perfect STAR' when you answer the question. They will have agreed an **ideal answer** to the question well in advance of the interview and will be asking the same or very similar questions of all the shortlisted candidates for the job.

So what sort of questions can you expect and is it possible to predict the likely questions that you will be asked at the interview? In most cases the answer is yes. Where the employer has actually identified the required competencies in the job advertisement it would be very surprising if they were not addressed at the interview.

Sometimes a little research will throw up the likely questions. If you have applied for the job through a recruitment agency then the recruitment consultant will most likely have been informed of the required competencies. In some cases they will know the actual questions that will be asked. Because competency interviewers ask the same questions of all the candidates the recruiter may be able to provide you with details of the actual questions that you will be asked, obtained from candidates who have already attended interviews for the same role. Using the example of the HR manager on the previous page, we can reasonably expect to have questions for each of the competencies listed in the advertisement.

Here are some examples:

Vision

- *'Can you tell us about a time when you translated your department's vision into a series of practical steps to achieve a particular objective?'*

- *'Can you give us an example of when you were responsible for implementing a major change within your department?'*

- *'Can we discuss a time when you were able to influence others to adopt your personal vision for the HR department?'*

Managing the business

- *'Can you give an example of a situation where you created and implemented new processes within your department?'*

- *'Can you illustrate how you implemented a framework to measure the performance of the people within your department?'*

- *'Tell us how you established and managed budgets within your department.'*

Leadership

- *'Can you tell us how you managed and motivated your team in your last role?'*

- *'Can you provide an example of a situation where you needed to turn around the poor performance of either an individual or a team within your department?'*

- *'Tell us about a time when you managed a large team of people from several different disciplines.'*

These are very typical examples of competency questions. It's useful to note how the questions are introduced and also that each of these questions can be answered very effectively using the STAR technique.

Trained interviewers will want to hear a full STAR in order to award maximum marks to your answer.

An example of a 'partial STAR', which would not be awarded full marks, would be the following response:

Question

'Can you tell us about a time when you introduced a new process within your organisation?'

Answer 1

'Well, I was working as HR manager at an investment bank. I reviewed the recruitment process and noted that it wasn't efficient. I decided to completely restructure the recruitment process.'

Unfortunately this answer will not be sufficient to impress the interviewers. It provides only the **situation** and the **task** but does not continue to provide details of the **action** that you took or the **result** of your actions.

Let's try again . . .

Answer 2

'Well, I was working as HR manager at an investment bank. I reviewed the recruitment process and noted that it wasn't efficient. I decided to completely restructure the recruitment process. I carried out a survey of the key stakeholders including all of the hiring managers within each department. I also carried out a review of the recruitment processes used by other investment banks. I then presented a very detailed plan to the head of HR at the bank and received formal approval to proceed. I introduced a new HR system based on Oracle HR and conducted a series of workshops to roll out the new processes across the business. As a result the recruitment process was much more efficient, more cost effective and resulted in measurably better hiring decisions with clear evidence that staff turnover was reduced by 15% over a 24-month period.'

That second answer would score full marks from the interviewer because it provides a full answer to the question and, most importantly, details the value added to the business in the positive result.

Be aware also that competency questions often lead to follow-up or probing questions. In the example of the HR manager, follow-up questions might include the following:

'How did you establish the recruiting practices of the other banks?'

'How did you measure the improvement in efficiency?'

You may also be asked competency questions even as someone applying for your first job. In the absence of any full-time work experience you will have to draw on your life experience or perhaps on any part-time or vacation jobs that you might have done.

Here's an example of a competency question for a graduate who does not have any previous work experience.

Question

'Can you tell us about a time when you had to complete a task or tasks to a strict deadline?'

Answer

'I was studying for my finals at university. I had several deadlines for the completion of assignments and also revision for the various final exams. I just had to get very organised as it would be so easy to miss a crucial date. I mapped out all the tasks that needed to be completed together with the relevant deadlines. I then worked backwards from the deadlines to calculate exactly how much time I had available for each task. I then scheduled all my activities to complete 24 hours before the deadline. This way I could plan all my work and still have some time to spare for any last-minute changes or revision. I actually managed to complete everything on time so I guess my system must have worked because I got a 2:i for my degree.'

Note that these examples follow the STAR format and demonstrate just how powerful the STAR model is for answering interview questions.

Competency questions tend to focus on *what* you did and the follow-up questions often focus on *how* you actually did it. Be prepared to answer both types of questions. These 'how' questions can catch out the unwary. Don't provide examples in your answers to competency questions if the work was mostly undertaken by members of your team and you have little idea of how the results were actually achieved.

Dealing with difficult questions

In addition to the questions that are typically asked at either traditional or competency interviews, you can also expect interviewers to focus on any areas of concern that they may have about your background, for example if you have changed jobs frequently or if there are any gaps in your career.

Here are some examples of these sorts of difficult questions with suggested responses.

'You've changed jobs quite frequently. How do we know that you are going to stay in this job?'

Well, this is a promising question. If the interviewer wants to be sure that you want to stay in the job then presumably they are thinking of actually offering you the job. But beware! Why *have* you been changing jobs so frequently? You need to reassure the interviewer with your answer.

'Yes, I have changed jobs several times but that has been a deliberate strategy. I wanted to gain experience in a number of different areas. I've come to the end of that process now and I can bring that experience to your company. I've also recently married and I want to settle down in a stable job. I've done a great deal of research on this company and I know that you can offer me job security and a long-term future.'

'You've been unemployed for quite a long time. What have you been doing?'

Try to give a detailed reply to this question. Remember that the average time to find a new job is 3–6 months. There are plenty of people in the same position and everybody knows that the job market is tough. You might also want to point out any personal projects that you have undertaken during your period of unemployment. If you were made redundant then you may have received a tax-free payment that enabled you to take some time off to travel or spend time with your family. If you have done any voluntary work then mention this and also mention any personal projects where you were able use your professional skills, for example acting as project manager for a property renovation or organising a charity event. Also mention any training that you have undertaken that will be relevant to the job.

Stress questions

Most people are very happy to be asked about their successes at interview; however, many interviewers who ask questions at either traditional or competency interviews sometimes like to question you about things that didn't go so well.

Examples would be the following.

'Tell us about a time when you had to deal with a customer complaint. How did you handle it?'

'Tell us about a time when you had to deal with a poorly performing member of your team? What actions did you take?'

Once again you can use STAR to answer these types of questions.

For example:

'A member of my team was performing badly and had failed to meet her financial targets for 3 months in a row. Her poor performance was starting to effect the morale of other members of my team so I had to take action immediately. I had a one-to-one meeting with the team member and quickly established that she was going through some difficult personal problems. She assured me that these would be resolved very shortly. Based on this information and on her previous good performance I offered her an immediate two weeks' paid vacation to sort out her personal problems. I asked for her assurance that once she returned she would concentrate 100% on her job and that I expected that she would hit her financial targets again. In fact, when she came back she managed to do very well and actually exceeded her financial target by 20%. She's still with my team now.'

Dealing with bizarre questions at 'extreme interviews'

'What colour is Wednesday?'
'How many bicycles were sold in the UK last year?'
'How do you weigh an elephant without a weighing machine?'

Yes, they're genuine interview questions! These rather bizarre types of questions are much favoured by university dons who are probably rather bored and decide to add a bit of spice into the interview process. But increasingly interviewers from outside the academic world are using these extreme interview questions just to see how you respond.

If you follow the advice given in this book then you will be very well prepared to answer most types of interview question. Of course, being well prepared is one of the key factors in interview success. But by using these types of questions interviewers are asking a question for which there can be no preparation. You can have no idea what kind of strange question the interviewer might ask. And that's just the point; the interviewer would like to see how you think on your feet and how you respond to something that is completely unexpected. There is some logic to this – dealing with unexpected situations might actually be a key requirement of the job. There's no *right* answer to these types of questions so my advice would be to relax and take the opportunity to have some fun and come up with the most amusing and memorable response you can. Spending a whole day interviewing candidates for a job can be tough and all of those 'perfect' candidate responses can sometimes become tedious. Make the interviewer's day and give a response that sticks in their mind. The chances are the interviewer will remember you and your response ahead of all the other candidates and you will have had the perfect opportunity to demonstrate that you can think on your feet, rise to a challenge, be funny and creative and, most importantly, deal effectively with the unexpected.

Illegal questions

Bizarre questions are one thing but sometimes the interviewer can overstep the mark and ask you questions that are actually illegal. There is strict legislation in the UK (and in many other countries) that means that questions about certain areas of your life are off limits at job interviews.

Questions about your ethnicity, religion or place of birth

Employers (and recruitment agencies) are required to confirm that you have the right to live and work in the UK; however, this question should be applied to all job applicants and not just to those with a foreign-sounding name. Employers can ask for information about your ethnicity on application forms but this should be used only for monitoring purposes. So questions like 'Where are you from *originally*?' are almost certainly illegal. If you have the right to work in the UK then your country of origin should have no bearing on your ability to do the job.

Your sexual orientation

The employer cannot ask any questions relating to your sexual orientation.

Your politics

Employers cannot question you about your political beliefs or about your membership of (legal) organisations.

Family life

Although it is normal for employers to ask about your marital status on an application form, an interviewer cannot question you about your family or, for example, about your plans to have children.

Age

There are now strict age discrimination laws in place. You do *not* need to put your age or date of birth on your CV or on a job application form. Questions about your age or when you plan to retire are not permitted. There are some exceptions to the age discrimination legislation and some jobs may legitimately have a maximum age requirement or indeed a minimum age requirement. Examples of these would be airline pilots, who are currently required to stop flying commercially at the age of 65, and young workers who may undertake only certain types of job until they reach school-leaving age.

Other types of selection activities

There's a lot of research that suggests that interviews alone are not the most reliable way of selecting the right candidates for jobs. The research suggests that individuals with good social skills can perform better at interviews and that less socially confident, but possibly more capable, candidates can get missed. For this reason employers often use a number of other selection activities. These activities are generally used to supplement interviews.

Work practice

Some employers now ask prospective candidates to spend a day or half a day actually working with the organisation doing the kinds of tasks that will form part of the job. This is your opportunity to shine and show the employer that you could be an important new member of their team.

Presentations

In addition to one of the interview types described above you may also be asked to make some kind of presentation as part of the selection process. Very often the subject of the presentation is not important; the employer wants to see how well you communicate and think on your feet. Presentations will be covered in detail in Chapter 7.

Assessment centres

Assessment centres are becoming much more common, particularly where the employer is looking to recruit a large number of staff. The assessment centre may consist of several different activities which are conducted during the course of a half day or full day of evaluation. Assessment centre activities are covered in detail in Chapter 8.

Psychometric assessments

Many employers are now using psychometric assessments to evaluate candidates. The assessments may include:

- a personality questionnaire
- a numerical reasoning test
- a verbal reasoning test
- inductive reasoning tests
- a variety of different aptitude and attitude tests.

What else will the interviewer(s) be looking for?

You may have prepared perfect answers to all the anticipated competency questions and carefully prepared answers about your background and qualifications, but you will find that there are a number of 'deal breakers' that will guarantee that you will *not* be offered the job. In other words, even if you are the perfect candidate in every other way, if you don't demonstrate these traits at interview you will be unlikely to succeed.

These critical areas are described below.

Your motivation

You must be able to show the employer that you *really* want the job. You need to show the interviewer your passion and enthusiasm. Remember that they will be investing considerable time and money to get you up to speed while you settle into the job. So make sure that you demonstrate your commitment not only by your answers to interview questions but also by the tone of your voice and your body language. One of the ways in which you can clearly demonstrate your commitment is by the amount of research that you have undertaken prior to the interview.

- You might print out key pages from the employer's website and take these with you to the interview.
- Obtain a copy of their brochure or catalogue of products and services and take these with you.

- Obtain a copy of the accounts if available.
- Find out at least one key piece of background information about the organisation and mention this at the interview.

If you are working in finance then it would be surprising if you didn't have information about an employer's accounts. If you are in sales then it would also be very surprising if you didn't have some information about the company's sales figures (if available) and their key products and services. The key here is to demonstrate to the interviewer that you have taken the trouble to undertake this level of research – this will most definitely confirm your motivation for the job.

Communication

You could be the best and brightest candidate interviewing for the job but if you can't communicate your ideas effectively you will not succeed. Good communication at interviews is not just about *what* you say but also about *how* you say it. Speak with real passion and make sure that you also use effective eye contact and body language to get your message across. Remember, good communication is also about listening. Demonstrate this by listening carefully to the questions being asked. Many interviewers complain that candidates don't listen to the question or don't answer the question. If you are not sure what is required, ask the interviewer to repeat the question. Make use of the STAR technique set out in Chapter 2 to describe your career achievements. Answering interview questions using the STAR technique will ensure that you communicate in a structured and clear way. Most interviewers will assume that if you answer their questions in such a structured way then this approach will also follow through into your everyday working practices. You can find out more about using the STAR technique at interviews on page 151.

Empathy

While it is important to be yourself at job interviews, you also need to be able to read the personalities and characters of your interviewers. Try to adopt an appropriate tone and ensure that the interviewers can feel that you will fit into the team and the company culture. Knowing something about your interviewers and the organisation prior to the interview will help you to do this.

Preparing your answers to interview questions based on the job advertisement

Apart from the common questions that have already been mentioned in this chapter you can also usefully spend some time trying to predict what questions will be asked at interview based on the job advertisement or job specification. Over the next few pages we'll examine three different jobs at different levels and see how best to prepare for the likely interview questions.

Example 1: bid manager

Look at this extract from a recent advertisement for a **bid manager**.

Essential skills and experience
- 5 years' (minimum) experience within the mobile telephony sector.
- Technical background in telecommunications (HND/degree).
- 3 years' (minimum) bid and tender management experience.
- Previous team management skills – leading and developing bid teams.
- A proven record of success in winning bids from clients within the mobile telephony sector.

A careful reading of the advertisement will help you to focus on the areas that the interviewers will almost certainly want to talk about at the interview.

Now look at the questions that you might expect when attending an interview for this type of role.

'Can you tell us about your commercial experience within the mobile telephony sector?'

You will need to highlight your specific commercial experience within this sector. Be prepared to answer questions exploring your in-depth knowledge of the sector. Who are the major players? What are the key commercial developments? What specific commercial success have you had in this sector? Who do you know?

'What's your technical background in mobile telecommunications?'

Self-explanatory, but don't talk at length about your technical expertise in areas that have no relevance for this particular employer. If you have done your research on the organisation then you will know the technical areas that will be relevant.

'Can you outline your experience in bid and tender management?'

Be prepared to provide full details of bids and tenders that you have managed. What was your level of responsibility? Did you respond to the original RFI or RFP? What support did you have? What was the size of the bid? How did you qualify the bid? Did you win the bid? If not, why not? What did you learn? Because this is a bid management role, the interviewer will almost certainly want to know about your specific revenue against target. Providing this is not commercially sensitive, so be prepared to bring specific data about your financial performance.

'What is your experience of managing a team?'

Questions in this area will almost certainly focus on your management style. In other words, *how* did you manage a team? What was the size of the team? How did you motivate and inspire the team? How did you deal with non-performance? Did you provide individual mentoring and coaching to members of your team? How would you measure the success of the team?

'Can you tell us about your experience of new business development?'

This suggests that the company is not interested in someone who can simply win bids with existing clients. They are clearly looking for someone who can generate new business. You will need to provide actual examples of your track record in new business development. How did you identify bid opportunities? Which clients? How did you win the business? What was the value of the new business?

'Can you tell us how you negotiate and build customer relationships?'

How do you manage customer relationships? How do you negotiate contracts with customers? Can you provide examples of specific contracts that you have negotiated? How did you deploy your communication skills to influence and enhance your customer relationships?

Example 2: office administrator
Let's now look at an advertisement for a position at a different level. Look at the extract below from an advertisement for an **office administrator**.

About you
- Huge amounts of confidence, first-class organisational skills and a genuinely flexible attitude are key skills for this office administrator position.
- Equal to your very proficient Word, Excel and administrative skills is your experience that has required a high degree of liaison, staff leadership, and working on projects within strict timeframes and budgets in customer-facing and busy, pressured environments.
- An aptitude for taking responsibility for delivering projects on time and to expected standards.
- Highly competent and able to demonstrate the ability to run several projects at any one time.

Again, this advertisement provides plenty of clues to the likely line of questioning during interviews for this role.

'Can you give us an example of a project that you have organised?'

Be prepared to provide actual examples of events or projects that you have organised. For example, have you managed an office move? Have you managed the reorganisation of the office floor plan or seating arrangements? Have you undertaken the procurement of new or upgraded office equipment? How did you manage this? How did you plan the event? Did you achieve your objective on schedule and within a set budget?

'Can you provide an example of your ability to adapt and be flexible at work?'

Being flexible means that you can cope with the ever-changing dynamics of a typical business. Try to give examples of situations where you had to demonstrate flexibility. Have you been temporarily assigned to a different role? Have you had to work from a different location for a short period of time? The interviewer will be looking for evidence of your ability to adapt and to fit in with the needs of the business.

'How would you rate your proficiency in Word and Excel? Can you provide examples of the kind of work you can do using these applications?'

You should consider taking examples of your work using Word and Excel. Take an Excel spreadsheet or Word report that you have created and show this to the interviewer. They won't have to read through the whole document to gain an understanding of your level of proficiency in these applications. If you are not confident in one of these applications then indicate what you are going to do about it. There are plenty of free or low-cost courses in both Word and Excel that are available as books, online or as a part-time course from a local institution.

'Tell us about your experience of staff leadership.'

How many staff have you led? What were their positions? How did you manage and motivate your team? How did you manage performance issues? How did you get the best out of your team? How would you get your team to work extra hours/days to complete an important project? For example, that office move might have required evening or weekend work – how did you accomplish this?

You should also be prepared to be given a scenario-type question. For example:

'We are planning to move to new and larger offices at another location to accommodate 100 additional staff. How would you go about planning and managing this project from start to finish against very tight deadlines?'

Typically there are four key factors in any project – scope, time, budget and resources. In this example you need to get a clear understanding of the scope of the project, i.e. exactly what will be involved. How far away is the new location? Will you be responsible for moving all the office contents including IT equipment? If the answer is yes then you may need specialist help. Will the IT manager be available? The deadline is tight but when exactly does the move have to be accomplished? How much time do you have? What's the budget for the move? Will you have control of the budget or will it have to be approved by someone else? Who is that person? What resources will you have? How many people will be available to assist you with the move? Can you request a number of reserve staff who may be willing to come in out of hours to help if other members of the team become unavailable or sick?

All of these questions will impress your interviewer and demonstrate that when it comes to projects you know what you are talking about and that you speak from experience. Apart from asking these questions, now would be a very good time to provide a specific example (perhaps using STAR) of a similar project that you have undertaken in your current role.

'How do you manage conflicting priorities at work?'

The job description refers to the need to manage 'several projects at any one time'. Do you have a specific example of this? How do you cope with conflicting priorities? Can you delegate? What would you do if one of the projects was falling behind schedule or running over budget? How would you manage if a critical member of your project team called in sick at a crucial time during the project?

TOTAL JOB SEARCH TIP

Use job advertisements to predict likely interview questions.

Example 3: personal assistant

Here is an advertisement for an entry-level position. Look at the extract from the advertisement for a **personal assistant** to work in the fashion industry.

This personal assistant position requires a candidate who is extremely professional, pays impeccable attention to detail and works effectively and efficiently within a dynamic environment. At times, this role will be demanding and challenging within a pressurised and competitive working environment, therefore it is critically important for the successful candidate to be organised and have the ability to multi-task while remaining calm and focused at all times.

- Advanced knowledge of MS Word, MS Excel, MS PowerPoint and MS Outlook.
- The ability to work in a team and autonomously.
- Impeccable attention to detail at all times.
- Outstanding organisational skills and the ability to multi-task.
- The ability to work under pressure.
- Knowledge of the fashion industry.

'Which is more important: meeting an important deadline or accuracy?'

Expect questions about work that you have undertaken where attention to detail has been critical. An interesting variation on this might be an example where detail is important but you are under pressure to meet a deadline. Which comes first: the deadline or the accuracy of the work? Would you call your boss and say that you need to have an extension of the deadline or deliver the work anyway? Would it make a difference if the work was internal or for a client?

'How do you cope with working in a pressurised and competitive environment?'

Of course, all businesses need to be very competitive and a pressurised working environment is usually the result. There will be tight deadlines and tough decisions. This typically means that you may have several, sometimes conflicting, priorities, with several pieces of work that all need to be completed by a specific time. Employers are looking for people who will understand the imperatives of winning business and putting the customer first. This competitive environment requires people who are prepared to go the extra mile and, if necessary, work late to meet a deadline. Have you got several good examples of this in your past experience? If this is your first job, can you give the example of meeting deadlines for exams at school or university? Most importantly, the employer will want to know that you can handle the pressure and that you are not going to collapse if it gets tough.

'Can you tell us about a time when you have had to complete a number of tasks by a strict deadline?'

Expect questions about your past experience of multi-tasking. Again, if you don't have actual work experience you can still use the example of exams at school or university; the key factors in multi-tasking are good planning and prioritising tasks. How do you plan your day to make best use of your time? How do you prioritise tasks? You may be given a scenario where you need to plan a number of tasks to be completed over a specified period of time. Can you delegate work to a colleague? Would you have the confidence to turn down (or renegotiate) the deadline for a task with a senior manager if you are working on something that you deem to be more important or urgent?

Here's a scenario.

'You are working on an important presentation for a client which must be completed before 5.00p.m. today. At 4.00p.m. a senior manager tells you to 'drop everything' to complete some work for her. What do you do?'

The correct answer is that the client presentation is going to be your first priority. You cannot break a promise to a client! However, this is the reality of multi-tasking. The senior manager's work is also important. Would you have the confidence to negotiate a solution with the senior manager? Could you delegate the work to a colleague? Could you undertake the work by staying late in the office this evening? You need to come up with a workable solution that will keep everybody happy.

'Do you work better on your own or as part of a team?'

Working effectively with other members of your team is going to be critical to your success in this role. If you have an excellent relationship with your fellow team members then you will be able to count on them to help you when that multi-tasking scenario arises. Equally, you need to be able to do the same for them. Team-working means actively cooperating with colleagues and going out of your way to help when required. At the same time employers want someone who is capable of working autonomously. Can you give an example of a situation where you have had to get up to speed very rapidly and work on your own to deliver an important piece of work? Can you work without supervision? Busy managers will not have time to support you all day. You need to be able to demonstrate that you are a self-starter who can plan and complete tasks without direct supervision.

'Please tell us how you would plan an important event.'

You can expect questions around your ability to organise and structure work. You may well be given a task or scenario, such as the following.

'Your boss is planning a meeting for 20 regional sales managers from other UK offices and from several countries in Europe. How would you go about organising that event?'

Think carefully before answering! This is a classic project and you will need answers to questions concerning the time line (when is the meeting), the venue, the budget, the resources (i.e. people to help you), etc. What the interviewer will want to hear is that you can think and plan in a structured way. Have you organised something similar? For example, did you plan or organise an event for your sports team at school or university? Have you planned any events like a large party or even a wedding? The interviewer will be interested in hearing about your actual organisational skills rather than a theoretical approach to this task.

'What do you know about the fashion industry? Who do you think are our major competitors?'

Do your research. Even if you haven't previously worked in the fashion industry you will still be able to demonstrate your knowledge. Read magazines, look on the internet, visit retail outlets. Understand where this particular business fits in the fashion industry. Who are their competitors? What are the key trends in their niche in the industry? What are the major challenges? Who are their customers? What are their current and potential markets? Even though this is an entry-level position for a graduate or school leaver, you will still be expected to show that you have a real understanding and, most importantly, a real passion for the fashion industry.

Practice makes perfect

We all know that the more you practise the better you will perform on an important occasion. So having carried out all your research, questioned the recruitment agency about the likely interview format and carefully analysed the job specification for likely questions, what else can you do to be well prepared for your interview?

The answer is to rehearse. If you have a video camera you can film yourself and then analyse your responses. Did you identify any gestures or mannerisms that might detract attention from your answers?

Have you got clear and succinct responses to these common interview questions that you can be almost certain will come up at any interview?

- Why do you want to work for us?
- What do you know about our organisation?
- How will you add value to our business?

In addition to these standard questions you might expect the interview to open with a gentle ice-breaker such as 'Tell us about yourself'. We've already referred to the **elevator pitch** in Chapter 4. You have 2 minutes to describe yourself, highlight your key skills and refer to some of your achievements. Don't improvise this on the day. What's important is to be clear, succinct and relevant. Don't spend half your allotted 2 minutes talking about a project that will have little relevance for this employer. If you have done your research you will already have matched your experience to the requirements of this job. You must *not* have a standard elevator pitch; it must be tailored to a specific job.

Deliver your responses to these questions to your video camera or to a family member or trusted friend who will provide you with constructive criticism and feedback. If you are not satisfied then keep practising!

Try writing out your answers to these questions for a job interview that you expect to attend shortly.

Question	Answer
Why do you want to work for us?	
What do you know about our organisation?	
How will you add value to our business?	

Using the job advertisement to predict specific interview questions

Look carefully at the job advertisement or job specification for *your* job interview. Now use this page to write down the specific questions that you expect to be asked and make notes or write down how you would answer the question.

Question	Answer

Attending the interview

Everybody knows that first impressions count and it's particularly true of job interviews. I know of several interviewers who have said something along the lines of 'I knew he wasn't right as soon as he walked through the door!' Unfortunately this kind of interviewing is all too common and judging someone in this way is a deeply unfair form of recruitment selection. If this ever happens to you then you can at least console yourself with the thought that you would not want to work for an organisation that employs someone who interviews in such an unprofessional way! However, it is true that first impressions do count and there is a lot that you can do to ensure that those first impressions are good impressions.

Making a great first impression

As advised earlier in this chapter, always dress smartly and professionally. Remember that your interview begins the moment you arrive at reception. Greet everyone politely and assume that each person you meet will be asked for their opinion of your conduct from the moment you enter the premises. When you enter the interview room do so with confidence. Remember the importance of a firm hand shake and good eye contact. During the interview be sure to listen carefully to the questions before answering and smile and make eye contact with everyone in the room. If there are several interviewers, try to engage with all the interviewers and not just the person who asked the question.

Answer the question
Don't waffle – stay on track! Try to answer clearly and succinctly. Try to be specific and don't assume that the interviewer is happy with your answer. Check their body language or ask if they would like a more detailed answer.

Remember it's about you!
If possible try to talk about your personal experience. Don't use 'we' if you can avoid it. The employer will want to know about your personal contribution, not that of your company or your boss or other members of your team. Try to

demonstrate the benefit you could bring to the organisation. Where possible give examples of your personal experience that exactly match the requirements of the job.

Ask your own questions

Take a notepad with you to make notes, and have some questions prepared and demonstrate your preparation by having them in front of you. I'll cover this in more detail later in the chapter (see page 175).

At the end of the interview

Before you leave the interview, confirm timescales and next steps, as well as how many other candidates are in the interview process – and remember to say thank you. You may also wish to follow up the interview with an email or letter thanking the interviewer and emphasising why you feel that you are the right person for the job.

How interviewers prepare for interviews

In this section we examine the different stages of a typical interview and note that there are distinct types of interview question that relate to each stage.

Here are some best practice guidelines given to interviewers with a large company on how to structure the beginning of a typical interview.

Guidelines for interviewers

- Greet the candidate.
- Settle the candidate.
- Introduce yourself and the panel.
- Provide a brief overview of the organisation.
- Provide a brief overview of the role.
- Describe the process of the interview.

You can see immediately that good interviewers want to settle you and make sure that you are comfortable before they start the actual interview. This is very much to your advantage as most people agree that they feel the most nervous during the first few minutes of an interview.

Good interviewers will also take some time to describe the organisation and give you an overview of the role. Hopefully you will already have done your research, but nevertheless you may learn something new here that may help you later in the interview. If appropriate you can indicate at this point that you have done a lot of preparatory work and that you are already aware of the key activities of the organisation and that you have carefully read through the job specification. This might also be the time to learn what the hiring manager is *really* looking for. As was mentioned before sometimes the job advertisement or job specification may not reveal all the requirements of the job. Here is your opportunity to hear all about the job directly from the hiring manager.

Good interviewers also describe the process of the interview. This can be very helpful and enables you to mentally prepare for the likely questions that you will be asked.

Once you have settled and have been briefed on the organisation and the job, it's now time for the proper interview to begin.

Prepare your own questions

It might seem that job interviews are all about you being *asked* the questions but in fact most interviews conclude with 'Do *you* have any questions?' Now, questions about holidays, working hours and overtime have their place, but they are certainly not the questions you should be asking at a first interview. It would be much better to think about some carefully crafted questions that will let the interviewer know that you have really done your research and are fully committed to the job. In fact it's fair to say that many interviewers attach a great deal of importance to the type of questions that *you* ask at the interview. And you don't have to wait until the end of the interview to do this. A great opening gambit to any interview is to ask the question:

'What are the key success factors for this job?'

It's not always possible to ask this question early on in the interview and of course the astute interviewer will simply turn the question around and ask you what *you* think the success factors are! However, if you do get an answer then you will know the agenda for the interview and you can start mentally preparing for questions about those specific areas. Additionally, you will have taken the initiative and demonstrated that you are thinking ahead and potentially taking control of the interview.

You could immediately follow up the interviewer's response and say:

'Let me address those points one by one.'

This approach may seem a little cheeky but I have sat in on a number of interviews where a forceful and confident individual has effectively taken control of the interview and, more importantly, has been offered the job. It's a risky strategy but if you have the confidence you might get away with it.

Much more likely will be the 'any questions' scenario at the end of the interview. These are questions that you can prepare prior to the interview and they are a powerful way for you to demonstrate your commitment to the job, your knowledge of the business and your motivation for the future.

So what sort of questions should you be asking?

Questions that demonstrate your knowledge of the organisation

You need to tailor your questions to the specific role that you are applying for. For example, as a job applicant for a sales role you might ask:

'I saw on your website that you are planning to open an office in New York. What impact will that have on your sales figures next year?'

If you are applying for a role in finance then you might ask:

'I noticed from your annual report that your **EBITDA** [earnings before interest, depreciation and amortisation] increased by 25% last year. Do you think you will be able to sustain that level of growth in the current market?'

For an administrative role an important question might be:

'I see that you have recently moved to larger premises. What challenges has the move presented to the administrative department?'

Always try to find some piece of inside information that will provide you with the basis of a question that will demonstrate your real interest and knowledge of the organisation. These types of questions will impress your interviewer.

Questions that demonstrate your commitment

'What kind of training is available?'
'How will you measure my success in the job after 12 months?'
'What are my long-term prospects with the business?'

The first two questions demonstrate that you are genuinely interested in the job. You want to obtain further training and you are interested in how your performance will be measured.

The third question clearly shows that you expect to stay with the company for an extended period of time. Of course, the actual questions that you ask need to be tailored to each interview. Don't make the mistake of inadvertently revealing your lack of preparation. For example, don't ask questions about topics that are clearly explained in the job advertisement or on the company website.

Questions about the culture of the organisation

'What kind of people succeed in your business?'
'Do members of the team mix socially after work?'
'Would I be free to manage my own work in this position?'

Each of these questions again demonstrates your interest and commitment to the job but also suggest that the organisation may need to sell the job to you as well. The third question in particular implies that you might not be interested in the job if you don't have an element of autonomy. If the interviewer starts extolling the virtues of working for their organisation then you've probably got the job!

It is most important not to say that you don't have *any* questions.

Most interviewers will view that as a negative point and it would tend to indicate that you are either not interested in or not committed to the job.

Try to prepare approximately 10 good questions before the interview. Some of them will probably be answered during the interview but you will still have some further questions to ask.

Finally, should you ask the cheeky question *'How did I do?'*

I've seen this work very well at a several interviews. You may get brushed off with:

'We've still got two more candidates to see.'

But you might also hear:

'Well we're slightly concerned about your lack of experience with Microsoft Excel.'

That one question was enough to turn around one interview from a rejection to a job offer. This particular candidate went on to ask:

If I agree to do an Excel course at my own expense will you offer me the job?'

The employer agreed.

TOTAL JOB SEARCH TIP

Prepare your own questions.

IN A NUTSHELL

- Do your research. Spend some time on the internet researching the organisation you are going to see. Don't get caught out by the question 'What do you know about us?'
- Don't be late! Make sure you have all the address details correct. If possible do a dry run of the journey at the same time as your interview. Plan to arrive at least 15 minutes before the interview starts.
- Dress smartly. If in doubt it's always safest to dress up for an interview. It's much better to be too smart than not smart enough.
- Carefully prepare your elevator pitch so that you can give a well structured response to the classic interview ice-breaker 'Tell us about yourself'.
- Practise your answers. Have a good look through the job specification or job advertisement before the interview. Try to work out what questions are most likely to come up and then practise your answers.

- Try to establish the competencies for the job before the interview. If possible, ask the recruitment agency or employer what these are.
- Listen to the interview questions. Remember that good communication is as much about listening as it is about speaking.
- Practise answering competency questions using the STAR format.
- Prepare your own questions. Ask smart questions that demonstrate your motivation and commitment.
- Use good non-verbal communication – strong eye contact, gestures and positive body language.

7 PRESENTATIONS

Most people don't associate presentations with their job search but increasingly employers are using a variety of different techniques to assess and select the right candidate for a job. These days candidates for jobs at every level are often asked to stand up and make a presentation. That's why it's so important for job hunters to feel confident to present, sometimes with little or no time for preparation.

This chapter will help you:

- understand why employers ask candidates to make presentations

- prepare for a short presentation at short notice

- plan and structure your presentation to maintain audience attention

- use visual aids and tools (such as PowerPoint) to add impact to your presentation.

Making a presentation

Giving a presentation is worrying for many people. In fact, in a number of different surveys of business people, **'giving a presentation'** was rated as one of the most stressful aspects of their work. In a survey conducted by *The Sunday Times,* 41% of people said that speaking in public was their 'biggest fear'. However, although it's human nature to feel nervous when presenting in front of a large group of people, with good planning and preparation, the nerves and anxiety can be overcome and it's important to remember that (most!) audiences want you to succeed. If you relax and demonstrate that you know your topic and that you have carefully planned your presentation then the audience will be on your side and willing you to succeed.

Presentations now play an increasingly important part in recruitment and selection. Job hunters can be asked to make presentations for jobs at every level – this practice is not just confined to senior roles. Graduate assessment centres and recruitment open days often include presentations as part of the selection process. However, making a presentation as part of an interview may require a slightly different approach to making a regular presentation. Generally, when you make a presentation as part of your job it will be about a subject in which you have considerable confidence. You could be making a presentation about your company's products or services or perhaps you will be making an internal presentation to colleagues or to the senior management of your organisation. But a presentation at a job interview may require you to present about a topic with which you are not especially familiar and may require you to present to an unresponsive audience of people you have never met before. Additionally, you may have very little or even no time for planning or preparation.

Another anomaly of the 'presentation for selection' is that the actual content of the presentation may not be important. Instead the interviewers (or selection panel) will want to see how you manage on your feet. They may deliberately interrupt your presentation or deliberately argue a point that you have made to see how you react under stress.

Even without time to prepare thoroughly there are still some key considerations that will help you to perform at your best. If you suspect that you will be asked to make a presentation then you can prepare a number of likely versions and then adapt them as appropriate at the interview. If you have applied for the job through a recruitment agency then the recruiter may be able to give you some idea of the likely interview format and whether or not a presentation might form part of the selection process.

Some typical interview presentation topics might include the following.

- Make a presentation about how you handled a similar job in the past.
- What would you do in your first 3 months in this job?
- Tell us why you are the right candidate for this job.
- Make a presentation about this company.

Assuming that you have at least some prior knowledge of the presentation topic then good planning is going to be one of the most important elements of your preparation. A key part of this planning is to research your audience. The research that you carried out on your interviewers will now also pay off at the presentation. Be sure to pitch your presentation at the right level so that the content is appropriate for your audience. Before a presentation try to find out the professional background of the participants and their familiarity with the topic you will be presenting. If you are going to be talking about a complex IT project and the audience will include the IT director but also the HR director and the finance director, then be sure to cover the personnel and financial elements of the project. It is most likely that you will be permitted some kind of visual aid for your presentation, whether it's a whiteboard or flip chart or ideally a laptop with PowerPoint. If you can create even simple visual aids prior to the presentation this will make a huge difference. You don't want to have to turn your back to the audience while you are writing on the board or flip chart.

Most good presenters use a very simple technique to plan and structure their presentation.

- Say what you are going to say.
- Say it.
- Say it again.

In practice this means that you should start off with an introduction stating the key points that you are going to cover in your presentation. You then need to cover each of those points in order. Finally you should summarise what you have said.

General guidelines for presentations

Have a powerful opening

When making a presentation it's very important to have a strong opening. You need to grab the attention of your audience within the first 10–20 seconds of a presentation. A hesitant or nervy start will almost certainly leave your audience feeling negative about the rest of the presentation. What can you do to grab the audience's attention? This very much depends on your audience and the content of your presentation.

Try these techniques.

Start your presentation by making a bold or controversial statement

'I can turn this problem around in 10 days.'
'50% of the people in this room are going to disagree with what I'm going to say.'

Tell a personal story

Everybody likes to hear a story that is told well. Starting your presentation with a story that illustrates exactly the point that you want to make may well capture the audience's attention. But make sure that the story relates to the problem or situation that is the topic of your presentation.

Tell a joke

This may be risky and you will need to carefully judge your audience, but a well told (and funny) joke is guaranteed to get the audience on your side. If they don't laugh then you might as well pack up and go home!

My advice? Unless you are very confident don't tell jokes.

Prepare

Good presenters are well prepared. Remember the maxim: *'Those who fail to prepare, prepare to fail.'*

Use visual aids

We have all heard the old adage that a 'picture speaks a thousand words'. Well it would be a very dull presentation that did not include some visual aids. You can use a computer with PowerPoint (or a similar presentation package) or you can choose to use a whiteboard or flip chart. The intention is to increase the interest of the audience and to enable you to summarise and illustrate what you are saying. Remember that visual aids can also act as a useful prompt for you to remember the key points of your presentation.

Practise

Once you have planned your presentation and put together some visual aids you would be well advised to practise. You could try this by yourself, maybe in front of the mirror (!) or even better with a friend, preferably a good friend, who will be able to give you constructive criticism. Apart from building your confidence, another reason to practise your presentation out loud is to check your timing. Very often you will find that you have a set amount of time for your presentation. Going on too long will mean that you may have to stop before you have made all of your points. Finishing too early probably indicates that you have not provided enough detail.

Dealing with nerves

If you find that you are nervous when you stand up to make your presentation there are several techniques that will help you.

- Practise, practise, practise!
- Know your material very well.
- Keep a small 'cue card' with the key points written down.
- Prepare – arrive in good time, set up any visual aids, etc.
- Smile and make eye contact with your audience.
- Speak with passion – put all your energy into your speech and your nerves will disappear.
- Speak up and speak clearly. Don't race through your presentation.
- Remember the audience want to hear what you have to say.

It's normal to feel nervous at first but once you get started the nerves will almost certainly settle down. Remember that it's not only you who feels nervous before a presentation. Even famous actors and politicians get nervous before going on stage or before an important speech. It's OK to be nervous; in fact, it's probably a good thing. You can use your nerves to give energy and impact to your presentation. Many presenters say that the adrenalin created from nerves makes them better performers on the day.

Learning your presentation

Some good presenters actually learn their presentation off by heart. If this works for you that's fine, and it has the advantage of ensuring that you cover all of your key points. However, some people might argue that you may lose some spontaneity by delivering your presentation in this way. It's your choice. Having a clear structure to your presentation (perhaps using STAR or a similar model) serves the dual purpose of keeping you on track and prompting you for the next points that you wish to make.

TOTAL JOB SEARCH TIP

Whatever you do, don't read the presentation!

Body language and non-verbal communication

It's important not only to sound confident but also to look confident. Never make a presentation sitting down (it happens) and try not to turn your back on your audience. This should never happen if you are using a computer for your presentation but even with a flip chart it should be possible to prepare most of your charts in advance and with a bit of practice you can then write or sketch on a flip chart while still engaging with your audience. Remember that 50% of communication is non-verbal. We communicate with our gestures, posture, eyes, body movements, facial expressions, smiling and so on. And, of course, our voice also conveys a tremendous amount to an audience – 'it's not what you say, it's how you say it' applies not only to the words we use but also to the pitch, tone, speed and volume that we use.

Remember to maintain eye contact with all the interviewers (or the selection panel) and don't address your presentation to a single individual. You should consciously 'sweep' the audience with your eyes and make clear eye contact with everyone throughout your presentation.

BODY LANGUAGE AND NON-VERBAL COMMUNICATION TIPS FOR AN EFFECTIVE PRESENTATION

- Try to relax and use open body language.
- Stand tall and try to face your audience – avoid turning your back to the audience if possible.
- Use gestures to emphasise key points but don't fidget or make fast or jerky movements.
- Try to vary the pitch of your voice.
- Don't speak too quickly.
- Don't mumble.
- Smile (but not too much!).

If you have the opportunity, use a video camera to check your presentation style. Get a trusted friend or colleague to comment on your speech, body language and gestures.

Taking questions

Ideally you should set your own ground rules at the beginning of your presentation and say clearly something like *'I intend to cover this topic very fully but of course I'll be happy to answer any questions at the end of the presentation'*. Unfortunately, interview panels tend to make their own rules and may well deliberately interrupt you to see how you react under stress.

The best preparation is to try to anticipate the likely questions (as you would in a job interview) and be fully prepared to answer those questions at any time during your presentation. Alternatively, if you are feeling confident and have carefully built the answers to anticipated questions into your presentation you can state firmly that you will be answering that question in detail later on.

Having a back-up plan

If things go wrong you need to have a back-up plan (or plan B). It's surprising how the best prepared presentations can sometimes fall apart because the presenter didn't have a well thought-out back-up plan. The sorts of things that quite commonly happen include the following.

- There's a power cut.
- The projector stops working or won't work with your laptop.
- There are no pens for the flip chart.

And so on.

We've all seen these sorts of disasters occur at other people's presentations and pray that they don't happen at ours!

If you have a power cut or cannot use your carefully prepared slides for any reason, then be sure to keep a printed copy of your presentation so that you can quickly write up your key points on either a flip chart or whiteboard. It's also a good idea to have sufficient print-outs of your slides to hand out *after* your presentation. Never give your audience copies of your slides or hand-outs *before* your presentation; you can guarantee that all the participants will be busily reading your notes rather than listening to you. Be sure to take spare whiteboard pens with you to avoid the problem of not having a back-up if the available pens don't work.

With technical failures (i.e. the projector doesn't work with your laptop) it's a good idea (if possible, and assuming you have prepared in advance) to send the presentation file to the employer (perhaps via the recruitment agency) with a request that the company sets up the presentation for you. This way the onus is on their technical team to have everything ready for you.

Organising your presentation

Let's assume that you have been asked to make a presentation (possibly at short notice) about a project that you managed in your previous job. This is a perfect opportunity for you to use the STAR technique to plan your presentation (for more on the STAR technique see page 46).

The situation

Begin your presentation by setting out the particular problem or business need that you were addressing with your project. If you are able to produce visual aids then a first slide or flip chart might set out the key elements of the situation. As a general rule try to avoid listing more than four or five items at a time. Audiences generally feel more comfortable if they know where you are going with your presentation so setting out the situation clearly at the outset is a very useful signpost that immediately informs the audience of the points you intend to cover. At this stage provide only brief details of the situation and make it clear that you will be addressing each point in more detail later. The best advice here would be to keep this introduction to your presentation brief and to the point. Remember that your objective should be to capture and hold your audience's attention.

The task

You've already described the situation that you faced; now you need to outline the actual tasks that you needed to perform in order to address the situation. Provide brief details of the tasks, perhaps counting them off on your hand or listing them on a slide or flip chart.

Action

Next you can describe the action(s) that you took to address the situation. Again, if possible write these on a flip chart or, even better, reveal them one by one on a PowerPoint slide. As you go through your presentation you can indicate each item on your list, making it easier for your audience to see where you are in your presentation and where you are going. These are critically important factors in holding your audience's attention.

Result(s)

Of course, this is the most important part of your presentation. You could perhaps refer back to the initial situation; remind the audience of the task that you had to perform and the actions that you took. Then you can go on to summarise the (successful) results of your project. If you are going to impress the interviewers then the story you tell in your presentation needs to have a happy ending.

Describe the success at the end of your project and, most importantly, the benefits for the business.

The STAR model works well for most presentations that describe a past event. However, you can still apply exactly the same model when talking about future events.

A very common presentation topic might be:

What would you do in your first 3 months in this job?

Looking to the future you could describe the current situation as you understand it, your view of the tasks that you will face in the first 3 months and the actions that you will take. Finally, you can describe the result that you *expect* to achieve at the end of that 3-month period.

Apart from STAR there are a number of other models that you can use to organise and structure your presentation. Some of the most commonly used models are outlined below.

Symptoms/cure

In this model you spell out all the **symptoms** of the current situation. For example, the team is performing badly, they haven't met their performance targets for the last 3 quarters, their morale is very poor and they are costing the company money. You then spell out the **cure**. Taking the symptoms one by one you map out your response to each of the problems.

- You carry out individual appraisals for the members of the team.
- You provide formal and informal training for the individuals who are performing badly.
- You review the performance targets and agree new realistic targets with the team.
- You put in place an attractive incentive scheme to reward high performers in the future.

This model can work very well for many different situations and has a narrative that the audience can follow easily. You set up the symptoms and the dire consequences of continuing along that path and everyone will want to hear what you are going to do to resolve the situation.

Critical analysis

In this model you identify a specific problem, perhaps with a business process or procedure. You analyse the problem and identify why it doesn't work effectively. You then provide the solution to the problem.

The analogy

This can be a very powerful way to describe a process or complicated procedure to an audience. For example, you could suggest that your first 3 months in the job will be like a visit to a doctor. First you'll examine the patient, carry out a number of tests and then prescribe the right medication to bring the 'patient' back to good health.

The chronological approach

If you are describing what you are going to do during the first 3 months in the job then the chronological model will work well. You can take each week or month separately so that you can describe a very structured step-by-step approach. During the first week you get to know the team, in the second week you carry out a review of the current situation, in the third week you arrange a series of one-to-one meetings with key stakeholders and so on.

Use an acronym

Just like STAR, an acronym can be a powerful way to organise a presentation and has the added advantage of providing a built-in prompt for what comes next. Good examples might include **SWOT**.

- **S**trengths
- **W**eaknesses
- **O**pportunities
- **T**hreats

The SWOT acronym could form the basis of a strong presentation examining the alternatives relating to a particular proposal or course of action.

IN A NUTSHELL

- Use a model such as STAR to structure your presentation.
- Know your audience.
- Know your material.
- Keep a small cue card with the key points written down to jog your memory.
- Be prepared – arrive in good time and set up any equipment or visual aids early.
- Smile and make eye contact with your audience.
- Speak with passion – put all your energy into your speech and your nerves will disappear.
- Speak clearly – don't gabble.
- Practise, practise, practise!
- Time your presentation.
- Prepare for questions from the audience.

8 ASSESSMENT CENTRES

The assessment centre is becoming a very common feature of recruitment and selection. It's often used as the first step in the recruitment of school leavers and graduates but it's also used increasingly as part of the selection process for more experienced job seekers.

Many candidates express concern about attending an assessment centre. This chapter sets out to clear up some of the misconceptions about assessment centres and explain what's actually involved.

This chapter will help you:

■ understand what to expect at a typical assessment centre

■ identify the different selection techniques that are used

■ become familiar with the different psychometric assessments and ability tests

■ perform at your best during the different assessment centre activities.

Background to assessment centres

Assessment centres are all about fitting round pegs in round holes. They can establish if you have the right personality attributes (or behaviours), skills and aptitude to perform well in a particular type of job. Think back to the profile of the air traffic controller who needs to be accurate and follow a set of rules. Those characteristics are essential for an air traffic controller but would not be appropriate for (say) an advertising manager who is paid to be creative and original, characteristics you would not want in an air traffic controller (at least not at work!).

It's very important to be clear that an assessment is not judgemental. There is no pass or fail; there are simply candidates who are well suited to particular types of job and candidates who are not. You certainly don't want to finish up being a square peg in a round hole, so the assessment centre is extremely helpful both for you and for your potential employer in ensuring that you don't work in a job for which you are unsuited. What's more, the results of the assessment centre may well be very helpful in directing you towards a job that *is* more suited to your particular set of skills and personality attributes. It is not unusual for candidates to be turned down for one particular role and then redirected towards another type of role with the same employer.

Despite all of the above, almost every time I mention to a candidate that there will be an assessment centre as part of the selection process I hear expressions of concern. It seems that everybody is worried about what those dreaded role plays and psychometric tests might reveal!

But do you really need to be so worried?

What is an assessment centre?

Assessment centres have been used as part of the candidate selection process for years. They are often used by employers who are planning to recruit a large number of staff, for example a large number of sales people or IT staff. They have also been used in graduate recruitment programmes with many blue-chip firms assessing potential bankers, accountants or lawyers over a full day's assessment. The armed forces have traditionally used assessment centres that sometimes take place over several days to select new recruits. It used to be the case that employers used assessment centres mainly for graduate-entry recruitment and for more junior staff, but increasingly companies are also using assessment centres to evaluate candidates for more senior roles.

The good news is that an assessment centre means that there will be a level playing field for all of the participants; after all, everybody is going to have to do the same exercises and tests as you. Assessment centres are also a sign that the employer has a structured and fair selection process. They are taking the selection of new staff seriously, and have invested time and money to ensure that only the right people are hired for the job. Much better than the worst types of interviews that are unstructured and where hiring decisions can be highly subjective.

Assessment centres sometimes come at the very end of the selection process but are more often the first stage of a structured series of interviews and selection procedures. Assessment centres are generally held over either a full day or a half day whereas a standard interview would generally be scheduled for just 1 or 2 hours. Employers will usually send out full details of the assessment activities in advance. If you are not sure if you will be attending just an interview or a full assessment it's always worth calling and checking what time the interview is expected to finish. A long session (i.e. more than 2 hours) would indicate that there will be other selection activities apart from the interview.

So what can you expect at an assessment centre? Find out more below.

Biographical or 'career history' interviews

We've already discussed competency-based interviews in depth and it may well be that a competency-based interview will form part of the assessment day. But you may also undergo a biographical interview which will be designed to test in detail your background and career history. Expect questions about your key skills, your strengths and weaknesses, qualifications and so on.

You can also expect questions about your personal motivation and personal circumstances. There may also be questions about your preferred work location, current salary and benefits, salary expectations and availability. These traditional-type interviews are also designed to discover any holes in your CV. Be very careful to make sure that you detail all the start and end dates of your various jobs in your CV. Astute interviewers will quickly uncover any gaps in your career history. If you do have a gap then honesty is the best policy; just state that you were made redundant, between jobs, or you took time off to renovate your house. It's not a crime and most people (including your interviewer) would probably also like to be able to take some time off for a personal project. The biographical interview may then lead into a competency-based interview so be prepared to use your STAR technique to answer those questions about your past behaviour.

Group exercises

A group exercise invariably involves a group of four to six candidates who are given a topic for discussion. There is usually some time allowed for preparation and then the assessors will sit in on your discussion. It's sometimes difficult to decide what role you should take within the group. If you are too assertive and dominate the discussion to the exclusion of the other members of the group, then this will almost certainly be viewed negatively by the assessors. Conversely, if you sit quietly and say nothing then they have nothing to assess! A happy medium is clearly the best path to take.

A very good technique, if you have the opportunity to speak to the other group members before the assessment begins, would be to try to establish roles for each member of the group. You might suggest the role of moderator or facilitator and then try to establish two sets of candidates who have opposing views. This way the group exercise can be structured like a debate and the topic covered in a structured way with equal time allocated to each member of the group. Depending on the nature of the job that you are applying for I would suggest that the facilitator is the role that will work best for you. This is particularly true if you can establish to the assessors that it was *your* suggestion that the different roles should be assigned.

Sometimes the assessors will actually assign roles to members of the group and the topic may be quite specific, for example whether or not a particular course of action should be taken based on a specific set of information. In these circumstances the best advice (again) is not to dominate the discussion and to listen to the other members of the group. Make sure you address all the members of the group when speaking and use appropriate body language and eye contact. Think of yourself in a normal business meeting; be courteous and invite comment from other members of the group. Apart from your actual behaviour and interaction the assessors will be looking at the way in which you structure an argument. Think of some of the models that were provided in the previous chapter on presentations, e.g. symptom/cure, critical analysis, SWOT and so on.

Role plays

Role plays are designed to assess your communication skills and, for example, your ability to engage with a client or key stakeholder in a given business scenario. You will generally be provided with information before the exercise; this may include details about the role that you will play, a description of the issue(s) to be discussed and some further data about the business.

Of course, the actual scenario will depend on the type of role that you are applying for, but recent examples that I have seen include the following:

- making a decision on whether to introduce an online support function for a particular product
- making a decision on the acquisition of another business based on a given set of financial data
- meeting with a client following a series of complaints relating to poor service levels.

Whatever the situation, the assessor will be looking for your ability to communicate well and to handle the situation effectively.

Presentations

We discussed presentations in some detail in the previous chapter. At an assessment centre you will most likely be asked to prepare a presentation around a topic related to the role that you are applying for. This could be focused on your proposed activities during the first 3–6 months in the job, for example, or could be related to a specific scenario as suggested in the section above on role plays.

Assuming that you have time to prepare, you should be able to use PowerPoint or a similar presentation package. My advice would be to prepare your presentation well in advance and then, if possible, email it either to your recruitment agency or to the employer direct, with a request for them to set it up on a laptop for you. As an added precaution (plan B) take your presentation on a memory stick or on your own laptop.

Of course, the PowerPoint slides are not the key focus of your presentation but they will help your presentation run more smoothly. You can also print out the presentation and leave copies with the assessors after the event. The assessors will also be looking at your delivery style and your ability to communicate effectively and think on your feet when answering questions.

Remember that timing will be a particularly important factor for a presentation at an assessment day. You may be one of many candidates being assessed and if the guidelines state that your presentation should be no more than 10 minutes then you do not want to overrun. Practise your presentation in advance using a video camera (or a friend, or both!). It's surprising how wrong you can be about the length of your presentation. With nerves, those 10 slides that you estimated would take 10 minutes could go much more quickly and you will finish up with time to spare.

In-tray exercises

These exercises are now often run using email, so you may find yourself seated at a computer with an inbox containing a number of emails from different people. You will then have to make decisions and potentially send emails based on the information that you have received and the sometimes contradictory information that continues to arrive in your inbox. In-tray exercises can be used with applicants for roles at every level. An exercise for a junior administrator might include a series of emails from colleagues or members of the management team with requests for information or instructions to do work that may conflict with work provided by another manager. You may need to decide how to prioritise or share work with a colleague. Another recent scenario involved an IT project that was running seriously behind schedule. With emails coming in from an irate customer, a stressed-out IT manager and your CEO, you need to make some rapid decisions to get things back on track. Assuming that you are an experienced IT project manager, this is almost certainly a situation that you will have dealt with before. Remember that the in-tray exercise is not designed to catch you out but simply to see how you would manage everyday situations at work. Nevertheless it's important to be accurate and respond appropriately to the customer, colleagues and the CEO.

Psychometric tests

The assessment centre may also include a number of different written tests. These tests are generally 'normed' against a group of individuals at the level of job you are applying for. If you are a senior manager then the norm group for senior managers will generally score at a particular level for that test. If you are applying for a more junior role then there will be a norm for that job level as well. Provided that you score within the range that is appropriate for the level of job that you are applying for, you will have passed the test.

Descriptions of the different types of ability tests

Most of the tests described on the following page could be categorised as 'ability tests'. They are designed to test your ability to perform successfully in a job. They cover a range of different skills including problem-solving and effective communication as well as assessing your creativity or ability to be innovative.

At your assessment centre you may be asked to undertake just one test or possibly a whole battery of tests to assess different aspects of your behaviour. Here are some examples of the different types of test that you may be asked to complete. Being familiar with the format of the tests will be an advantage. Visit www.shldirect.com/practice_tests.html where you can practise full-length examples of these tests.

The following descriptions are for tests that are used most frequently by employers in the UK. Other test providers will have very similar tests, all of which have to meet the demanding standards set by the British Psychological Society or other authoritative bodies around the world.

General cognitive ability tests

Verbal reasoning tests
These tests measure your ability to interpret written information and to assess arguments about the information.

Verbal comprehension tests
Verbal comprehension tests are designed to assess your ability to interpret and understand written information.

Numerical reasoning tests
These types of tests focus on statistical and numerical data and your ability to interpret the information based on the data presented in a number of different formats.

Inductive reasoning tests
Inductive reasoning tests are designed to assess your ability to work with unfamiliar information and find conceptual solutions through analysis of the information provided.

Situational judgement tests
Situational judgement tests assess your ability to make good judgements based on situations or scenarios in the workplace. You may be presented with a number of different options and asked to select the most effective solution.

Accuracy tests

As the title suggests, these tests assess your ability to detect errors in a given piece of information quickly and accurately.

Personality questionnaires

If you are given a personality questionnaire (sometimes called an occupational personality questionnaire or OPQ) this will often consist of a number of statements that require you to indicate which behaviour is *most like you* and *least like you*. The advice usually given to candidates is not to think too hard about your responses. Usually the first instinctive response is actually the most accurate. Remember also that these are *occupational* questionnaires and they are not designed to examine your personal life; they are specifically designed to establish your likely behaviour in the workplace. Don't try and manipulate your answers or try and be someone you aren't. Most personality questionnaires have a built-in system to spot inconsistent answers. Honesty is the best policy, so just be yourself.

General advice for completing cognitive ability tests

While I don't believe that you can improve your natural performance in taking cognitive ability tests, you can practise taking all of the tests listed above. If you are not familiar with them then a couple of hours spent practising will at least familiarise you with the likely format and the type of questions that you can expect. Being prepared and knowing what to expect should enable you to relax and complete the tests to the best of your ability on the day.

If you are faced with a numerical reasoning test there are a number of things that you can do to ensure that you perform to the best of your ability. These tests generally last for about 20–25 minutes and the challenge is not so much the difficulty of the questions but the time that you have available to complete them. If there are 25 minutes and 25 questions then you have only 1 minute per question.

Some tests will permit you to choose which questions to complete first, so you might want to consider looking very quickly for any 'easy' or very straightforward questions first and then moving on to the more difficult questions later. Unfortunately some test publishers do not give you this option and you need to work through the questions in a set order. If it looks like you are going over time on a particular question then it may be worth just moving on to the next question and, if possible, returning to the difficult question later. If you cannot work out the answer at all then consider a calculated guess (rather than a calculation). If there are four multiple choice answers you have a 25% chance of being correct!

If you cannot determine the order in which you answer the questions, then it will be even more important to manage your time efficiently. It is very difficult to complete all the questions in the allocated time and you need to be very strict with yourself.

Lots of employers use tests developed by the same test provider, so following on from my earlier advice to learn something from every interview or selection process, use your experience of taking a test. Even if you are not successful, you may receive the same (or at least a similar) test the next time you attend an assessment centre.

The same advice can apply to the other ability tests, including the verbal reasoning tests that are commonly administered at assessment centres. Answer the easiest questions first and carefully monitor the time that you spend on each question. Follow the SHL link given on page 203 and you will find a free resource where you can practise these tests.

General guidelines for assessment centres

Assessment centres are sometimes run a long way from your home address. They may be held in a central location so that they are accessible for the majority of people attending. Assessment centres also generally start early in the morning. Ask if the employer will provide you with hotel accommodation the night before. Having a very early start is not the best preparation for a gruelling day of assessments and staying in a hotel close to the venue the night before will enable you to at least start the day feeling refreshed.

Remember that you will be assessed on your performance *throughout* the day. That means that you will not be assessed only on the set activities but also on your behaviour during breaks and mealtimes. Are you sitting alone during breaks or are you making a positive effort to engage with the other candidates (perhaps your future colleagues) and also with the assessors. Here is your opportunity to demonstrate the preparation you have undertaken and your knowledge of the business. A lunchtime chat with one of the assessors might also reveal some useful advice on how to behave at one of the afternoon's activities.

It's also important to remember that the wide range of activities covered during an assessment day mean that you probably won't perform well on every exercise. So don't be disheartened if you feel that you have not performed at your best on a particular activity. You will probably be assessed on your overall performance rather than on your performance on that specific exercise.

Don't worry too much about assessment centres – they are not as daunting as you might expect, and even if you don't get offered the job you will come away better prepared for the next time and with some interesting feedback on your personality at work and your performance on the various exercises and ability tests. All of this will enable you to be better prepared on the next occasion.

IN A NUTSHELL

- Remember that assessment centres are designed to match you to a job that suits your abilities and personal attributes.
- You can't improve your innate abilities but you can practise the tests so that you are at least familiar with their format.
- When completing personality questionnaires don't try to 'change' your personality. Usually your first, instinctive answer is the right answer for you.
- Try to find out about the likely activities well before the assessment centre. Ask your recruitment agency or the employer if they can provide further information. Some online

employment forums contain information from candidates who have previously attended an assessment centre with that employer. But beware: the activities or topics for role play or discussion will almost certainly be different at each assessment centre.

- Ask the employer to provide you with hotel accommodation the night before the assessment centre if the location is a long way from your home.
- If you have a topic for a presentation then prepare well in advance and either take your laptop or a memory stick with your presentation with you or, even better, ask the employer to set up the presentation file for you.
- Remember that you may be assessed over the whole day, including your behaviour at mealtimes and during breaks.
- Be active, be friendly, participate and be yourself.
- If you are not selected, learn from the experience so that you perform even better on the next occasion.

9 NEGOTIATING A JOB OFFER AND STARTING YOUR NEW JOB

Although you've almost reached your objective there are still a couple more hurdles to jump. You need to make sure that all of the terms and conditions being offered by your new employer are fully acceptable. If they're not then you will need to start the delicate process of negotiating the terms before formally accepting the job offer. And then (if you are still working) you will need to resign from your current job with the minimum amount of disruption to the business while considering any potential counter offers that might persuade you to stay where you are.

This chapter will help you:

■ understand the importance of stating your salary and benefit requirements at the beginning of your job search

- negotiate or renegotiate the terms and conditions offered by your new employer

- resign from your current job

- ensure that you will receive the best possible references from your referees

- develop a plan to make the first few months in your new job a success.

Reviewing a job offer

You have attended the assessment centre and interviews and you have been offered the job. Congratulations! You have done extremely well to be offered a job in the current difficult job market. However, there are still some issues that you may wish to address before you actually accept the offer.

Take some time to look through the offer in detail. It's important not to look at the headline salary figure. A job offer will have several different components that you should consider carefully before accepting. So don't just accept an offer at the end of a final interview. Be polite and enthusiastic but ask for all the details in writing. Be very careful; it is not unheard of for an employer to withdraw an offer simply because you didn't accept immediately. You need to find a balance between maintaining your enthusiasm and letting the employer know that you are extremely interested in the job but not committing yourself fully until you have seen all the details in writing. If you are still working, under no circumstances should you resign from your current job until you have a firm (and acceptable) offer in writing.

So what are the factors that you should consider when reviewing a job offer?

There may be a number of personal factors to consider, such as the following.

- Is the job location convenient? If the job will require an expensive commute will that wipe out any possible increase in salary?
- Are the working conditions to your liking? For example, the possibility of flexible working hours and so on.

You should also think about how your acceptance of this job offer will take you forward in your career. How will accepting this particular job and working for this particular company look on your CV when you come to change jobs in a few years' time? If the job is quite different to anything that you have done before then that might represent an exciting challenge for you now but might also make it difficult for you to get back into your main career in the future. Is the company operating in the same sector as your previous employer? Again, moving into a completely new sector might be exciting and challenging but could make it more difficult to return to your previous sector when you are next looking for a job.

The other important areas of the job offer that should concern you are:

- the salary and benefits package (of course)
- the bonus (if any)
- the likely trial period (if any)
- the terms of the employment contract
- your job title
- the reporting line (who you will report to)
- your reports (i.e. the people reporting to you).

In addition to these key points you will also need to negotiate your departure from your current job (assuming you are still working) and ensure that you retain all of your contractual entitlements from that job.

The salary and benefits package

It's vitally important that you make your salary requirements very clear to either the employer or the recruitment consultant at the time that you first apply for the job. Now is not the time to discover that your hard-fought job search has been in vain and the salary offered is much lower than you had expected. Being absolutely clear and specific about your salary and package requirements from the initial application is important, and yet it is not unusual for the actual offer to be different from what you had expected. Of course, there could be a number of elements that will still make this offer acceptable to you. If the job is very close to your home and will therefore save you time and money when commuting then that is certainly one good reason to consider a slightly lower salary. It may be that the salary is lower but the benefits package more than compensates for the reduction. For example, a fully expensed company car or full medical cover for you and your family would be benefits that have a real monetary value. Similarly, additional vacation days or a more generous pension contribution are both factors that you should consider alongside the actual salary. In addition to the basic salary there may be a bonus that will be payable. Is this a figure that you could reasonably expect to receive, assuming that it is based on your own performance (which you can control), or is it paid on the basis of company performance (which you may not be able to control)? If the latter, then you would be wise not to take this into consideration when comparing salary packages.

What can you do if the offer is unacceptable?

If you are fully satisfied with all the components of the job offer then go ahead and accept. But what should you do if you find that there are parts of the offer that are not acceptable? Bear in mind that the employer should have been made aware of your expectations at the time that you applied for the job so in theory there should be a reasonable match between your expectations and the actual offer.

But what if there isn't?

Of course, you could simply walk away and continue your job search, but after all this effort, and assuming that you really do want the job, you should carefully consider your next move.

As soon as you have made the decision that the offer is not acceptable (in its present form) you should contact either the recruitment consultant (if you applied for the job though a recruitment agency) or the employer direct. Rather than simply rejecting the offer your initial response should be to establish whether there is any flexibility on the offer. Again, it's very important to demonstrate your enthusiasm and commitment to the job. At this point the employer may come back with an improved offer or ask how much more you are looking for. If you were quite clear about your salary expectations at the time of application then you can simply state that you are looking for the figure that you originally requested. If, despite your request for an improved offer, the salary remains unchanged then you will have to negotiate.

Step one negotiation tactics

- Calculate your absolute bottom line, taking into consideration all the elements of the offer and not just the basic salary.
- Set a minimum figure which you will accept. You must be prepared to walk away if this figure is not met.
- Go back to the employer with that figure (+10% to allow for some further negotiation).
- Make sure that you are realistic in your salary expectations.

If the employer still won't (or can't) move on the basic salary then you have to either walk away or try to negotiate other elements of the remuneration package.

Step two negotiation tactics

- Ask for the bonus (if available) to be guaranteed in the first year.
- Try to negotiate on the personal benefits, for example to extend individual medical cover to family cover.
- Request a better-quality (or more economical) company car.
- Ask for a free season ticket for your travel or an interest-free season ticket loan.
- Ask for an early salary review. With most organisations this review takes place annually but it may be possible to have a review sooner, perhaps immediately after successful completion of your trial period.

Resigning from your current employer

You've struck a deal and you have an acceptable offer from your new employer. The next step (assuming you are still working) is to inform your current employer that you are leaving and to ensure that your departure is handled professionally and seamlessly. Ideally you would like to hand in your notice and continue to be paid up to the point when you start work for your new employer. Additionally, you want to depart on good terms and ensure that you receive an excellent reference. Remember that job offers are often 'subject to satisfactory references' so this is an extremely important factor.

In my experience the best way to resign from any job is to do it in person. Don't just send an email or letter. It is much better to make an appointment with your manager and explain that you have been offered another job and that you intend to accept the offer. If possible (and if appropriate) you should reassure the manager that you will work out your contractual notice period if required and that you are ready and willing to hand over the job and if necessary participate in the search for a replacement. The purpose of this meeting is to reassure the manager that there will be minimal disruption and that you are prepared to do everything possible to ensure a smooth handover. Follow up the meeting with a formal letter of resignation.

What if I receive a counter offer?

It is sometimes the case that when you hand in your resignation your employer offers you an increased salary to stay. You may well feel very flattered to receive this offer of more money. You could of course accept immediately and congratulate yourself on getting an unexpected pay rise and the opportunity to continue working for the same organisation and with the same familiar colleagues. However, perhaps you should ask yourself why you wanted to leave the job in the first place. Was it really just the money or were there other aspects of the job that were not to your liking? Was handing in your resignation really the only way to get a pay rise? The reality is that if you went to all the trouble of searching and applying for another job and going through all the interviews you must have really wanted to change jobs. Bear in mind that if you decide to stay and accept the counter offer you may nevertheless be viewed with suspicion by your bosses who may take a dim view of the fact that you have obtained a job offer from another (possibly competitive) organisation. Yes, you have your pay rise now but how will this fact affect your future with the company? Furthermore, the reason that your employer has offered you a pay rise may not be entirely benevolent. After all, it's very inconvenient to lose an employee unexpectedly; there will be a substantial cost attached to finding and selecting a replacement and possibly an expensive recruitment agency fee to be paid. Offering you a little more money might just be the cheapest option for your manager. The fact is that counter offers very rarely work out. Despite having some extra money all the frustrations that caused you to look for another job in the first place will probably still be there. So, unless you receive a very substantial pay rise, my advice is to decline the counter offer and go ahead and take the new job.

One further consideration is that accepting a job with a company and then going back and announcing that you have changed your mind does not send out a great message to your industry. It's a small world and word does get around. Changing your mind in this way may leave the impression that you are not a reliable or decisive individual. That's certainly not a message that you want to be attached to you in future job searches.

Preparing to start your new job

You've resisted any potential counter offers and you have a firm written offer from your new employer, which you have accepted. That offer may be 'subject to satisfactory references' so now is the time to make sure that all your referees are ready and willing to provide you with a good reference. If feasible you should actually speak to all your referees and also provide them with full details of your new job, including the original job advertisement or job specification. You might also take the opportunity to brief your referees on why you think you are particularly well suited to this new job and perhaps remind them of some of your past achievements that helped you to win the job.

At this time you should also start monitoring the 'on-boarding' process with your new employer. It's surprising how many new employees turn up on the first day at work only to find that their new boss is away on vacation and there is no desk, company car, mobile phone or laptop in place. It really does happen. Assuming you haven't been reassured that all these things are in place, you could diplomatically approach the HR department and ask for details.

TIPS FOR SUCCESS IN YOUR NEW JOB

- Clarify your goals for the first 3–6 months.
- Confirm how your performance will be measured.
- Make a point of being friendly and approachable.
- Start networking within the new organisation – plan to make at least five new friendly contacts in your first week (i.e. people who can help you).
- Start as you intend to continue.

The key areas to discuss should be:

- confirmed first meeting with your new boss
- the arrangements for your company induction
- your work location (which may be different from the venue for your interview)
- parking arrangements (if any)
- your security pass or details of who you should ask for on the first day
- details of your company vehicle (available on the first day?)
- details of your company mobile phone, including the number if available
- details and availability of your company laptop.

Some people get stressed about starting a new job – it's not surprising considering that you will be working in a new location with people that you don't know and in a working culture that may be quite different to your previous employer. A good way to reduce your stress levels is to make a plan for how you are going to manage the early days in the new job and get clear direction from your new employer on what will be expected of you and, most importantly, on how your performance will be measured over the first 3–6 months of your employment.

Congratulations! You have achieved your job search objective!

IN A NUTSHELL

- Don't formally accept a job offer without first carefully checking the terms and conditions.
- If an offer is not acceptable then go back to the employer and try to negotiate an improved package.
- If the employer will not (or cannot) move on the basic salary, look for other areas of the package that can be negotiated including bonuses, benefits and the salary review.
- Always resign in a face-to-face meeting with your current employer.
- Make sure you carefully consider the implications of accepting a counter offer.

- Inform your referees that they are likely to be contacted and if necessary brief them on your new job.
- Stay close to your new employer and ensure that your 'on-boarding' has been properly planned.
- Structure the first few months in your new job.

10 RESOURCES

Recommended reading

You're Hired! CV: How to write a brilliant CV (Corinne Mills)

You're Hired! Interview: Tips and techniques for a brilliant interview (Judi James)

You're Hired! Interview Answers: Brilliant answers to tough interview questions (Ceri Roderick and Stephan Lucks)

You're Hired! Psychometric Tests: Proven tactics to help you pass (Ceri Roderick and James Meachin)

You're Hired! Assessment Centres: Essential advice for peak performance (Ceri Roderick)

Free online resources for practising psychometric tests

www.shldirect.com/practice_tests.html
Free advice on assessments and the various psychometric ability tests. You can take (free) full-length practice tests on this site. While you cannot improve your innate abilities, practice will make you more familiar with the format of the tests and enable you to perform at your best when you take the actual test.

http://practicetests.cubiks.com
Another site where you can become familiar with how online psychometric tests work and get some free practice (and feedback) before you complete the real thing.

Free online resources for obtaining careers advice

https://nationalcareersservice.direct.gov.uk/Pages/Home.aspx
The UK government's National Careers Service provides advice for job hunters at every level. Includes useful tools to help you make the right choices at the beginning of your career.

www.nidirect.gov.uk/get-free-learning-and-careers-advice (for Northern Ireland)
More free careers advice from the UK government. If you are considering a career change or returning to work, this site has excellent advice on learning opportunities and the most suitable qualifications and training.

Online forums where you can exchange information with other job hunters

http://careers.guardian.co.uk
Combine your job search with an online forum where you can also obtain career-related advice, guidance and news.

www.forums.learnist.org
A job seekers' forum covering everything from CVs to application forms and interview preparation.

Competency statements

Here are some examples of short competency statements that are commonly required for management jobs. You can adapt them to match your own professional background.

Strategic management. Proven ability to make a positive medium- and long-term impact by drawing up coherent strategic plans, sometimes based on incomplete or ambiguous information. Developing the corporate vision.

Leadership. Managing and motivating high-performing multi-disciplined teams. Ensuring effective performance management of the teams via meaningful goal-setting, feedback and coaching.

Budget management. Responsible for project budgets of up to $12 million. Effective management of third party resources and external vendors and suppliers.

Customer relationship management. A focus on managing key client relationships and the negotiation of contracts. Further responsibility for quickly establishing trusting client relationships and assuring the fulfilment of contractual obligations.

Project management. Hands-on experience of managing the full life cycle of projects. A qualified project management professional (PMP).

Commercial focus. An entrepreneurial flair and a strong commercial awareness. Identifying opportunities for increased revenues. Offering specialist financial advice to ensure optimal business decision-making.

Business change. Real expertise in initiating fundamental change relating to both the market and operating model of a number of large, complex organisations. Managing change in order to respond rapidly to market dynamics.

Organisational development. Provides expertise in support of reorganisation, restructure and business growth in line with the strategic needs of the business.

Networking. Selects key business partners and establishes strategic alliances with the objective of growing the business and identifying new business opportunities leading to increased revenues.

Business development. Works alongside the business development teams to identify new opportunities and develops and manages a network of senior-level relationships with customers and potential customers.

Communication. Strong communication skills. Proven ability to interact at every level within an organisation and to communicate effectively with both financial and non-financial managers.

Motivated. A highly motivated individual with excellent analytical and problem-solving skills and a proven ability to deliver against key business metrics.

Action words that can add impact to the achievements in your CV

Achieved	Developed	Persuaded
Administered	Devised	Planned
Advised	Diagnosed	Presented
Analysed	Discovered	Promoted
Arranged	Distributed	Recommended
Assessed	Evaluated	Represented
Budgeted	Examined	Researched
Calculated	Explained	Selected
Completed	Instructed	Sold
Conducted	Liaised	Solved
Controlled	Managed	Supervised
Coordinated	Monitored	Taught
Created	Negotiated	Tested
Designed	Organised	Trained

Recruitment agencies

There are hundreds of recruitment agencies in the UK. We cannot take responsibility for the performance of individual agencies, but this selective list includes agencies that are members of the Recruitment and Employment

Confederation (REC). Agencies marked with an asterisk (*) are past winners or runners-up in the annual Recruiter Awards for Excellence, which are nominated by both employers and recruiters.

Recruitment agencies that cover a range of different job categories and sectors

Adecco www.adecco.co.uk

Amoria Bond * www.amoriabond.com

Blue Arrow * www.bluearrow.co.uk

Eden Brown * www.edenbrown.com

Finegreen Associates * www.finegreen.co.uk

Harvey Nash www.harveynash.com

Hays www.hays.com

Hudson www.hudson.com

Huxley Associates http://uk.huxley.com

Hydrogen * www.hydrogengroup.com

Manpower www.manpower.co.uk

Michael Page www.michaelpage.com

Morgan McKinley * www.morganmckinley.co.uk

Oliver James Associates www.ojassociates.com

Reed www.reed.co.uk

Regan and Dean www.regananddean.co.uk

Robert Walters www.robertwalters.com

Tangent International www.tanint.com

The Curve Group * www.thecurvegroup.co.uk

The Synergy Group www.synergygroup.co.uk

TMP Worldwide www.tmpw.co.uk

Volt Europe * www.volt.eu.com

Recruitment agencies for IT, telecommunications and networking jobs

Astbury Marsden * www.astburymarsden.com

Computer Futures www.computerfutures.com

Computer People www.computerpeople.co.uk

ConSol Partners * http://consolpartners.com

Glotel * www.glotel.co.uk

Henderson Scott * www.hscott.co.uk

IT Human Resources * www.ithr.co.uk

La Fosse Associates www.lafosse.com
Matchtech * www.matchtech.com
Networkers International * www.networkersplc.com
Nicoll Curtin * www.nicollcurtin.com
Penta Consulting * www.pentaconsulting.com
Randstad Technologies www.randstadtechnologies.com
The JM Group * www.thejmgroup.com
Vector Resourcing www.vector-uk.com

Recruitment agencies for graduate jobs

Bateman Carter www.batemancarter.com
Best Graduates www.best-graduates.co.uk
Bright Futures www.brightfutures.co.uk
Cooper Jones www.cooper-jones.co.uk
FreshMinds Talent www.freshmindstalent.co.uk
GradJobs www.gradjobs.co.uk
Inspiring Interns www.inspiringinterns.com
Pareto www.pareto.co.uk
The Graduate Recruitment Company www.graduate-recruitment.co.uk

Recruitment agencies for jobs in HR

Annapurna HR * www.annapurna-hr.com
Ashdown Group www.ashdowngroup.com
Frazer Jones www.frazerjones.com
Hays www.hays.co.uk
Hudson www.hudson.com
Michael Page www.michaelpage.co.uk
Oakleaf Partnership www.oakleafpartnership.com
Ortus www.ortushr.co.uk
Reed www.reed.co.uk

Recruitment agencies for jobs in banking and finance

Addeco * www.adecco.co.uk
Astbury Marsden * www.astburymarsden.com
Austin Benn www.austinbenn.co.uk
Badenoch & Clark www.badenochandclark.com
Barbara Houghton Associates www.bhal.co.uk

Citifocus www.citifocus.co.uk

Goodman Masson www.goodmanmasson.com

Hays www.hays.co.uk/banking

Hays * www.hays.co.uk/financial services

Huxley Associates www.huxley.com

LMA Recruitment www.lmarecruitment.com

Marks Sattin * www.markssattin.co.uk

NJF Search * www.njfsearch.com

Oliver James Associates * www.ojassociates.com

Randstad Financial & Professional * www.randstadfp.com

Robert Half International www.roberthalf.co.uk

Selby Jennings * www.selbyjennings.com

Walker Hamill www.walkerhamill.com

Watson Moore * www.watsonmoore.com

Recruitment agencies for jobs in retail

360 Resourcing Solutions * www.360resourcing.co.uk

Detail2Retail * www.detail2retail.com

Elite Associates * www.eliteassociates.co.uk

Exsurgo * www.exsurgo-group.com

McCarthy Recruitment * www.mccarthyrecruitment.com

Quest Search and Selection * www.questsearch.co.uk

Randstad Retail www.randstad.co.uk

Recruitment agencies for secretarial and office jobs

Adecco www.adecco.co.uk

Attic Recruitment www.atticrecruitment.co.uk

Carlton Recruitment www.carlton-recruitment.com

Office Angels www.office-angels.com

Reed www.reed.co.uk

Tate www.tate.co.uk

Recruitment agencies for sales and marketing jobs

Austin Benn www.austinbenn.co.uk

Brand Republic www.brandrepublic.com

Direct Experience www.direct-experience.com

Matchking www.matchking.co.uk

The Spice Partnership www.spicepartnership.com

Recruitment agencies for teaching jobs

Beacon Education www.beaconeducation.co.uk

Capita Education Resourcing www.capitaresourcing.co.uk

Career Teachers * www.careerteachers.co.uk

Classroom www.classroomteachers.co.uk

Connaught Education www.connaughteducation.com

Impact Teachers * www.impactteachers.com

Protocol Education www.protocol-education.com

School Staffing * www.schoolstaffing.co.uk

TimePlan www.timeplan.com

Trust Education www.trusteducation.co.uk

Recruitment agencies for technical, engineering and oil and gas jobs

Air Energi www.airenergi.com

AndersElite * www.anderselite.com

CBSbutler * www.cbsbutler.com

Earthstaff * www.earthstaff.com

Matchtech * www.matchtech.com

NES Global Talent * www.nesglobaltalent.com

Recruitment agencies for international jobs

Antal International * www.antal.com

NES Global Talent * www.nesglobaltalent.com

Penta Consulting * www.pentaconsulting.com

Robert Walters * www.robertwalters.com

RP International * www.rpint.com

Recruitment agencies for healthcare and pharmaceutical jobs

Carrot Pharma Recruitment * www.carrotpharma.co.uk

Medic International * www.medicinternational.co.uk

The Pathology Group * www.pathologygroup.co.uk

Your World * www.yourworldhealthcare.co.uk

UK internet job sites

General job sites
www.jobserve.com

www.jobsite.co.uk

www.monster.co.uk

www.reed.co.uk

www.totaljobs.com

Specialist job sites
www.allexecutivejobs.com (executive-level jobs)

www.caterer.com

www.cityjobs.com

www.cwjobs.co.uk (IT jobs)

www.efinancialcareers.co.uk

www.exec-appointments.com (senior executive jobs)

www.justengineers.net

www.netjobs.com

www.onlymarketingjobs.com

www.theitjobboard.co.uk

Aggregate job sites (which search multiple job sites)
www.fish4.co.uk

www.indeed.co.uk

www.simplyhired.co.uk

www.workhound.co.uk

UK headhunters

Note that headhunters do not generally accept direct approaches from job hunters; however, some do advertise vacancies on their websites. Assuming you find a suitable vacancy, then of course a direct approach is permissible.

Heidrick & Struggles www.heidrick.com

Korn/Ferry International www.kornferry.com

Odgers Berndtson www.odgersberndtson.co.uk

Spencer Stuart www.spencerstuart.co.uk

Zygos www.zygos.com

Job advertisements in the national press

Newspapers advertise vacancies both in the hard-copy newspapers and also on their websites. Note that some newspapers advertise particular categories of jobs on different days of the week.

Sector	Monday	Tuesday	Wednesday	Thursday	Saturday	Sunday
Business and finance			Independent	Times Telegraph		Observer
Creative and media	Guardian	Independent		Times		
Education and research		Guardian Times		Times Independent		
IT	Independent			Guardian Times		Observer
Sales and marketing	Guardian	Independent		Times Telegraph		
Public sector		Times	Guardian	Telegraph		Telegraph
Science, engineering and technology		Telegraph		Guardian Telegraph		
Job supplement				Times Telegraph	Guardian	Observer Sunday Times

The following newspapers have dedicated careers sections on their websites that also advertise jobs in different categories and at all levels, including entry-level jobs for school leavers and graduates.

Guardian – http://jobs.guardian.co.uk/profile

Telegraph – http://jobs.telegraph.co.uk

The Times – http://appointments.thesundaytimes.co.uk/cvmatch